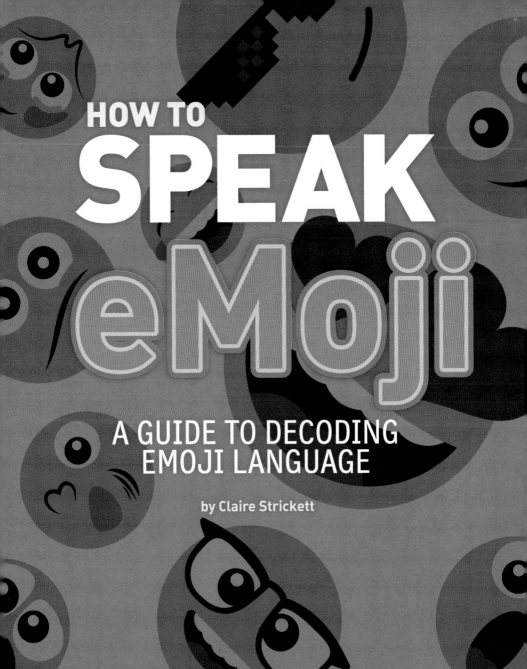

HOW TO
SPEAK
eMoji

A GUIDE TO DECODING
EMOJI LANGUAGE

by Claire Strickett

**NATIONAL
GEOGRAPHIC**
WASHINGTON, D.C.

CONTENTS

Emojis...

EMOJIS HAVE TAKEN over the world—there's no doubt about it.

These tiny symbols burst into our lives only a decade ago, but now they're everywhere you look. You'll find them in text messages, on social media, on T-shirts and furnishings—even in museums, in poetry, and starring on the big screen!

But where did they come from, how did they become so popular, and, most importantly of all—what do they mean?

Emojis have changed the way we communicate, and given us entirely new ways to express ourselves. But this also means that they've created new ways for us to get confused, or be misunderstood.

With the help of this book, you may never be confused by a message from a friend again —and you'll be well on your way to being fluent in emoji.

MEET THE author

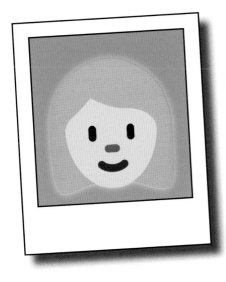

CLAIRE STRICKETT studied languages, literature and translation at university (although sadly there were no classes in emojis on offer). She has worked as a writer and in marketing, social media and advertising, and is based in London. Her favourite emoji is 😐 and the emoji she most wishes existed but doesn't (yet!) is a ginger version of 💁.

FOR YOUR SAFETY

WHETHER YOU'RE SENDING a message on WhatsApp to a friend, posting a status update on Facebook, tweeting on Twitter, or just browsing the internet, it's very important to consider your online safety at all times. Make sure you follow these tips for staying safe when communicating with emojis.

NEVER POST personal information, like your address or mobile number online. Decide carefully what you *do* post online. Once you've uploaded something like a photo, other people may be able to see it forever—even if you remove it.

DON'T GIVE OUT your passwords to anyone—not even your best friend. For maximum security, make sure your passwords use a combination of upper and lower case letters, numbers and symbols, and ensure your social media account settings are set to maximum privacy.

SOMETIMES people pretend. Don't take it for granted that anyone you talk to online is who they say they are.

The history
OF EMOJIS

Emojis were
born in
Japan
in 1999.

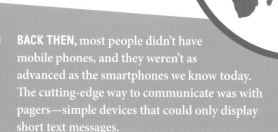

BACK THEN, most people didn't have mobile phones, and they weren't as advanced as the smartphones we know today. The cutting-edge way to communicate was with pagers—simple devices that could only display short text messages.

A SOFTWARE engineer called Shigetaka Kurita is usually called "the father of emojis". He noticed how much people around him liked using images (as well as written words) to share their thoughts and feelings with each other. He realised that if he created small pictures or symbols that could be sent by pager, that would make his pager company stand out from the competition. And with that, emojis were born!

Shigetaka Kurita

THE NAME 'emoji' comes from the Japanese words *e* ('picture') and *moji* ('character' or 'letter'). It's a complete coincidence that it sounds like the English word 'emotion' even though it's true that emojis are often used to share our feelings.

'emoji' in Japanese

THE FIRST emojis were much simpler than the ones we know today, and there were a lot fewer of them. What's more, because they were created in Japan, among the first emojis were plenty of symbols relevant to Japanese culture that can look mysterious or strange to people from other countries. (If you've ever wondered why there was a sushi emoji long before there was a cheese emoji—well, it's because sushi is much more popular than cheese in Japan!)

sushi emoji

IT WAS really thanks to the launch of Apple's iPhone that emojis began to take over the world. At first, Apple only included emojis in the Japanese version of their software. It wasn't long before iPhone owners in America stumbled across the emojis buried on their phones. They were too good not to use, so in 2011 they were made available to everyone—and the rest is history!

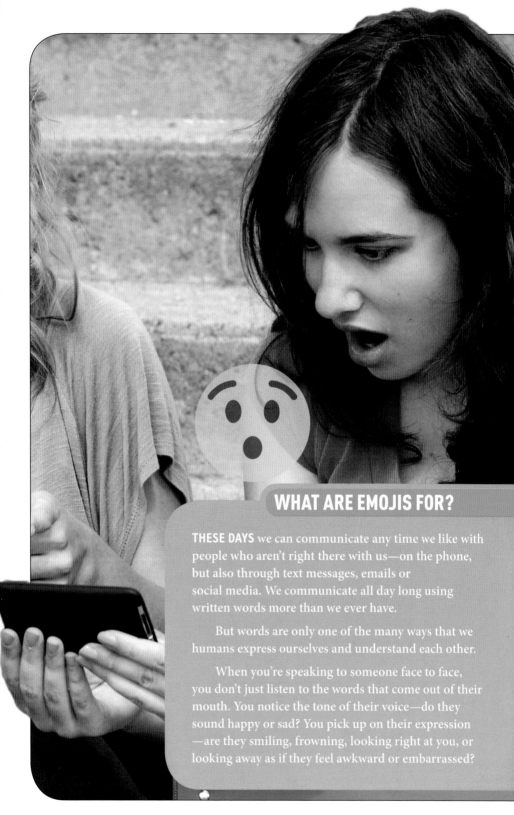

WHAT ARE EMOJIS FOR?

THESE DAYS we can communicate any time we like with people who aren't right there with us—on the phone, but also through text messages, emails or social media. We communicate all day long using written words more than we ever have.

But words are only one of the many ways that we humans express ourselves and understand each other.

When you're speaking to someone face to face, you don't just listen to the words that come out of their mouth. You notice the tone of their voice—do they sound happy or sad? You pick up on their expression —are they smiling, frowning, looking right at you, or looking away as if they feel awkward or embarrassed?

Body language

WE HUMANS are amazing at reading body language. In fact, scientists estimate that between 60–90% of what we communicate when we're face to face happens without using words at all.

So it's hardly surprising that when we send each other messages that only contain words, we feel like there's something missing.

We can emphasise the most important word in a sentence—the way we would with our voice if we were speaking. We can show what kind of mood we're in, without having to describe it using more words, and without anyone seeing our face.

MOST OF THE TIME, emojis aren't replacements for words—they work alongside words to enhance their meaning, so we can make ourselves even better understood.

I can't believe he did that!

I know, I have no idea why... 😕

hmmm—give me a minute to think about that

HOWEVER, because we so often communicate with each other while we're busy and on the move, emojis can sometimes be useful shortcuts. After all... why take the time to type a whole word when an emoji will do?

SIGNS and SYMBOLS throughout HISTORY

EMOJIS MAY HAVE ONLY BEEN INVENTED in the late 1990s, but we've been using images to communicate for a lot longer than that!

 ## THE WRITING'S ON THE WALL

ON THE WALLS OF CAVES across the world, archaeologists have discovered pictures and symbols left there by people who lived long ago. The earliest, in Spain, are more than 40,000 years old!

Are these the ancient equivalent of emojis? We'll never know exactly why our ancestors created these images. They weren't purely decorative, that's for sure—many are found in parts of caves that would have been extremely hard to reach. Different archaeologists have made different suggestions—many suspect that the cave paintings were thought to have magical powers!

No matter where in the world these cave paintings were made, they tend to have similar themes—pictures of animals (such as bison, bulls and deer) are especially popular, as were handprints.

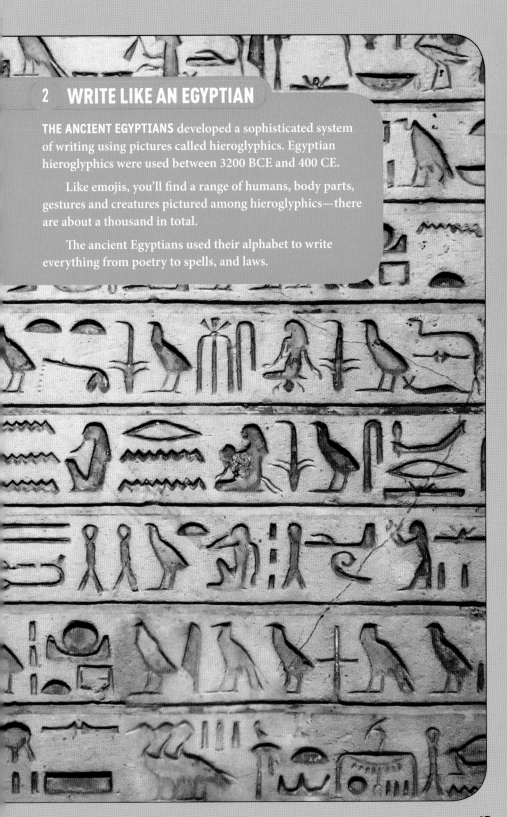

2 WRITE LIKE AN EGYPTIAN

THE ANCIENT EGYPTIANS developed a sophisticated system of writing using pictures called hieroglyphics. Egyptian hieroglyphics were used between 3200 BCE and 400 CE.

Like emojis, you'll find a range of humans, body parts, gestures and creatures pictured among hieroglyphics—there are about a thousand in total.

The ancient Egyptians used their alphabet to write everything from poetry to spells, and laws.

MYSTERIA MISSUS, SUPPRIO
IS DEINDE PASTOR, ET ZELO
O IN GRAMMASTETTEN OVI
NDE PROFANO PASTORE CY
E DONATUS, CANDIDO HILARI
, QUOT IPSE SACRAS OVES
SUPERIORIS AUSTRIÆ BIS D
TIBUS NON VENTIS VERBA, S
TATE, AC DULCEDINE SUA, V
DA RAPUIT, NON PRÆDO
ULIVS, SED SINGULIS IDEM,
OS UT FILIOS PIUS PARENS
OMNIA BENE VIDIT, MELIUS
OVAVIT

EDIBUS
DINIS,
AUT A
R FAC
NANE
NEM
ABRI
PLEN
ÆE FUNDATÆ D

3 AS EASY AS ABC

AN ALPHABET LIKE THE ANCIENT EGYPTIAN ONE—where symbols represent words or phrases instead of a sound—is called a 'logographic system'—from the Greek words *logos*, meaning 'word', and *graphikos*, meaning 'drawn' or 'written'.

Over time, the ancient Egyptians began to use hieroglyphics to represent not just individual ideas, but individual sounds—just like our alphabet today.

In our modern English alphabet, symbols—letters—don't represent a particular idea or thing the way emojis do. They represent sounds. We call this a 'true alphabet'. By combining letters, we can recreate the sounds of different words, which give us the meanings familiar to us from spoken language.

4 GIVE ME A SIGN

BUT OF COURSE, although we now have our modern alphabetical system, written words aren't the only things we read.

Our world is full of systems of pictures, images and colours that carry meaning without using a single word—just like emojis.

Next time you're travelling along a road, look out for the traffic lights and the pedestrian crossings. You don't need words to understand that red means stop and green means go.

Or take a look at the remote control that you use to control your television or stereo. The ⏻, ▶, and ▶▶ symbols probably all make instant sense to you—but you don't need to read a single word. You may not even have ever stopped to think about how you make sense of these shapes, colours and signs.

It's often only when we visit a different country or culture that we realise there's nothing 'natural' or 'normal' about the signs and symbols we take for granted.

In Europe, red is a sign of danger and negativity, but in China, people 'read' the colour red as a sign of celebration and good luck. And in South Africa, red is associated with death and mourning—much the same way the colour black is in Europe. Even apparently simple, instinctive, visual ways of communicating are often much less simple than we think.

5 AND THEN THERE WERE EMOJIS...

THE END OF THE 20TH CENTURY saw the birth of emojis! Go back to pages 8–9 for more information.

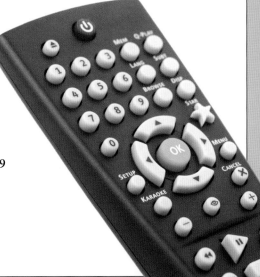

PROCESSING LANGUAGE

WE KNOW WHAT VISUAL communication, such as emojis, looks like. But how do our brains process it?

Some studies have analysed brain activity when participants looked at emojis and found that we don't necessarily interpret them in the same way we would recognise familiar faces, but that we associate them with an emotion. As some of the first emojis, and the most enduringly popular ones, have depicted smiling faces, it shows that emojis are used not only to represent a physical object or feature, but to express how the user is feeling.

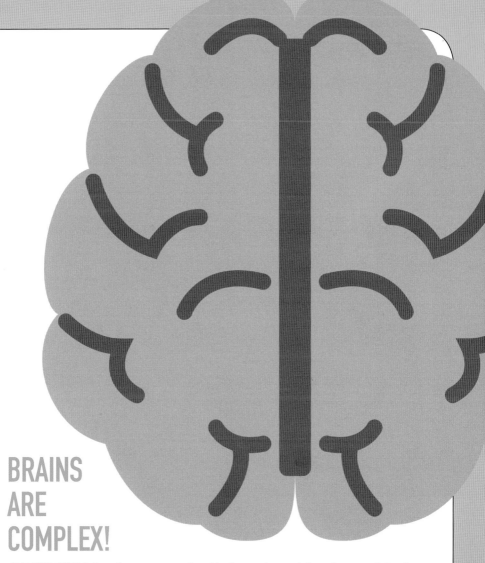

BRAINS ARE COMPLEX!

DID YOU KNOW that they process visual information quicker than text? Or that the majority of the information processed by the brain is visual?

This is why, if you've ever used a study chart or mind map, it may help you to take in information and remember it more easily than simply reading it. This is also why presentations at school and in the workplace often contain slides with pictures, or why a teacher might draw on a blackboard.

Emojis are fun to use, but visual symbols are used across the world in many different ways to get a message across quickly and clearly—from street signs to traffic lights, safety warnings and menu symbols, visual symbols are all around you. Throughout this book, you'll find a few examples of visual communication used both for fun and for practical purposes.

Rolling on the floor laughing

Smileys

HOW ARE YOU FEELING?

Whatever the answer, there's bound to be a smiley for it.

These round, yellow faces are the classic emojis. There are hundreds of the little critters, expressing every emotion from joy to misery. Even though they're called smileys, some aren't smiling: they're crying, frowning... or don't have a mouth at all!

Before smileys, there were 'emoticons'—simple ways to add expressions to messages using punctuation. From :-) to ;-) to :-(and many more, these proto-emojis were once the only way we had to show how we felt using a keyboard.

Although the two words sound similar, it's just a coincidence—go back to page 9 for more information.

Although smileys don't look like real people, thanks to their bright yellow 'skin', having simple features and no hair, it's usually easy to understand what emotion a smiley is expressing. However, some are a little bit more mysterious, so it's important to get to know your smileys.

MOST-USED EMOJI

FACE WITH TEARS OF LAUGHTER is officially the most popular emoji in the world, according to studies by Twitter and Facebook.

FACE WITH TEARS OF LAUGHTER

This face is laughing so hard it's crying tears of laughter—the emoji equivalent of 'LOL', or 'laughing out loud'.

EXAMPLE: You said what?!

SMILING SWEATING FACE

This combination of a wide grin with a bead of sweat is used to show relief—phew!

EXAMPLE: It's all good 😅 My keys were in my pocket all along!

ROLLING ON THE FLOOR LAUGHING

This face is laughing so hard, it's rolling on the floor—the emoji equivalent of 'ROFL' or 'rolling on the floor laughing'.

EXAMPLE: I am 🤣 right now!

WIDE GRINNING FACE

Smiling eyes and a wide smile make this emoji ideal for expressing joy and excitement.

EXAMPLE: It's the weekend! 😄

WINKING FACE

This cheeky winking face makes it clear that someone's only teasing, and shouldn't be taken too seriously. It can also be a sign that someone's feeling flirty!

EXAMPLE: That hat REALLY suits you 😉

ROSY-CHEEKED SMILE

With its broad smile and smiling eyes, this emoji is used when someone's feeling as happy as can be.

EXAMPLE: I'm so happy to hear from you

BEFORE EMOJIS, emotions were often expressed using punctuation marks. Match the emotions expressed with punctuation marks from the blue box with an emoji from the orange box. Answers are on page 172.

1. :-)   2. :-P   3. ;-)   4. :-(5. :'-(

a. 😛   b. 😉   c. 😢   d. 🙂   e. 😞

FACE WEARING SUNGLASSES

A smiling face sporting a pair of shades. Used to show that everything's cool, or that someone feels chilled.

EXAMPLE: Exam went well 😎

GREEDY FACE

This face is licking its lips in anticipation—usually of something delicious to eat, but by extension, anything someone's looking forward to.

EXAMPLE: Already thinking about what to order when we get home 😋

KISSING FACE WITH HEART

This cheeky face is winking and blowing a kiss—used to show love and affection for someone.

EXAMPLE: I love you, Mum 😘

HEART-EYED FACE

A grinning face with hearts for eyes, this emoji means 'I love it' or 'looking great!'

EXAMPLE: Just seen your new hair!

SMILEY FACE

The classic smiling emoji, with a contented look and big, open eyes.

EXAMPLE: Honestly, no worries at all

KISSING / WHISTLING FACE

This kissing face also looks like it's whistling, so it can be used to show that someone's killing time.

EXAMPLE: Still waiting for that answer from you...

HUGGING / TA-DA FACE

This happy face has its hands held out in front of it. It's used to represent a hug, joy, or with the sense of 'ta-da!'

EXAMPLE: My treat

LOOK AT THE MESSAGES IN THE ORANGE BOX.
Choose the best emoji from the blue box to match each message.
Answers are on page 172.

1. That dress is gorgeous!
2. I could NOT hide my amusement!
3. All ready for a relaxing holiday.

a.
b.
c.

23

NEUTRAL FACE

This face has expressionless eyes and a straight mouth—it's often used when someone doesn't know how to react, or doesn't have much to say.

EXAMPLE: I guess there's nothing else we can do about it 😐

CHIN STROKE FACE

This emoji is stroking its chin thoughtfully—the equivalent of 'Hmmm!'. Often used to react in a sceptical or doubtful way, or just to say 'let me think about it'.

EXAMPLE: Go on...? 🤔

FACE WITHOUT A MOUTH

With wide eyes and no mouth at all this emoji is often used to show that someone is speechless, or choosing to stay quiet.

EXAMPLE: I won't breathe a word 😶

BLANK FACE

With blank eyes and a straight mouth, this emoji looks totally blank. It's usually used to mean 'no comment', or to show disappointment or sulkiness.

EXAMPLE: Everyone else is invited… and I'm not

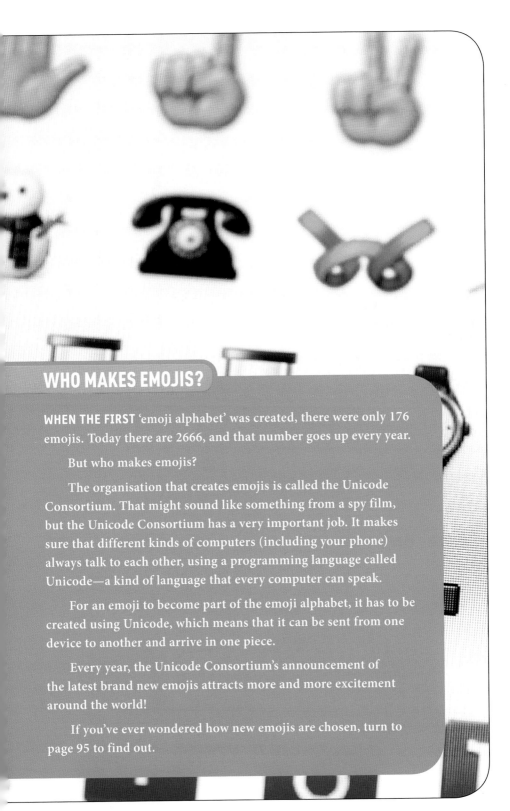

WHO MAKES EMOJIS?

WHEN THE FIRST 'emoji alphabet' was created, there were only 176 emojis. Today there are 2666, and that number goes up every year.

But who makes emojis?

The organisation that creates emojis is called the Unicode Consortium. That might sound like something from a spy film, but the Unicode Consortium has a very important job. It makes sure that different kinds of computers (including your phone) always talk to each other, using a programming language called Unicode—a kind of language that every computer can speak.

For an emoji to become part of the emoji alphabet, it has to be created using Unicode, which means that it can be sent from one device to another and arrive in one piece.

Every year, the Unicode Consortium's announcement of the latest brand new emojis attracts more and more excitement around the world!

If you've ever wondered how new emojis are chosen, turn to page 95 to find out.

SMIRKING FACE

This sideways smirking emoji is used to indicate that someone feels smug, or that they are in on a joke.

EXAMPLE:

Oh yeah, of COURSE it was an accident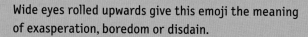

ROLLING EYES FACE

Wide eyes rolled upwards give this emoji the meaning of exasperation, boredom or disdain.

EXAMPLE:

Can't believe she did that

SURPRISED FACE

This face's wide open mouth is used to signal surprise—sometimes sarcastically.

EXAMPLE:

I really wasn't expecting him to react how he did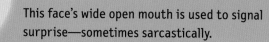

ZIPPED MOUTH

With a fastened zip in place of its mouth, this emoji is used either to ask someone to keep a secret, or to promise to keep quiet.

EXAMPLE:

Your secret's safe with me

BACK IN THE DAY...

BACK IN 1887, the American writer Ambrose Bierce made the case for a symbol that could be included alongside written text to show that the writer was being ironic or joking. It looked something like a) turned on its side to form a smile. If only he had lived long enough to use emojis!

SHOCKED FACE

With raised eyebrows and a wide mouth, this face means someone's shocked.

EXAMPLE: Hang on, he said what?

SLEEPY FACE

This weary emoji has a 'sleep bubble' coming out of one nostril—a traditional Japanese Manga way to show someone's asleep. As this isn't common outside Japanese culture, it's usually seen as a tear, and used to show weary sadness.

EXAMPLE: Ergh, I've had enough of this

LOOK AT THE MESSAGE IN THE BLUE BOX. Choose the best option from the orange box to translate it. The answer is on page 172.

  that I am

a. So sad that I am sweating.

b. So exhausted that I am crying.

c. So angry that I am soaked.

EXHAUSTED FACE

Similar to the 'sleepy face' (see page 27), this emoji looks defeated and exhausted.

EXAMPLE: 10pm and I'm still doing homework

SNORING FACE

A sleeping face that's letting out a gentle snore—used to indicate tiredness or boredom.

EXAMPLE: What a day! I'm off to bed

CONTENTED FACE

This peacefully happy face shows relief or contentment.

EXAMPLE: Thank you, you shouldn't have!

FACE WITH STUCK-OUT TONGUE

With its tongue sticking cheekily out, this emoji shows that someone is only joking and that what they're saying shouldn't be taken seriously.

EXAMPLE: Sorry not sorry

DROOLING FACE

This emoji's mouth is watering in reaction to something irresistible—sometimes literally food, but by extension the thought of anything desirable.

EXAMPLE: OMG, need!

UNAMUSED FACE

This unamused, unimpressed face is used to react unfavourably to something.

EXAMPLE: That's exactly what they said last time

SAD SWEATING FACE

With its anxious frown and a bead of sweat on its forehead, this emoji indicates stress, or sometimes illness.

EXAMPLE: All this work is getting to me

DOWNCAST FACE

This sorrowful face is used to show overwhelming sadness and sympathy.

EXAMPLE: That's terrible

CONFUSED FACE

With its mouth turned down and blank eyes, this emoji is used when someone isn't sure how to react—but it definitely isn't good.

EXAMPLE: I don't know much about it

UPSIDE DOWN SMILE

This mysterious emoji can be used in a wide range of ways. It can be used as a sign of sarcasm, or in a passive-aggressive way to show someone isn't really happy—just pretending to be.

EXAMPLE: That's fine

BACK IN THE DAY...

SMILING YELLOW FACES were a part of our world for a long time before emojis were invented. A simple yellow smiley face image first appeared in the early 1960s. Since then it's appeared on T-shirts, car-bumper stickers, keyrings and anything else you can imagine!

These smiling yellow faces also became the face of a Scottish campaign. In the 1980s, the search was on for a slogan to promote Scotland's largest city, Glasgow, in order to encourage tourism and boost the local economy. The 'Glasgow's Miles Better' slogan (a play on 'smiles'—'*Glasgow smiles better*') quickly became associated with Mr Happy, the 'Mr Men' character—and by extension, any smiling yellow face!

Glasgow

SORROWFUL FACE

With its sad, downcast look, this emoji represents feeling sad and defeated.

EXAMPLE: There was nothing I could do...

WORRIED FACE

This emoji's raised eyebrows and downward-turned mouth are used to show worry or fear.

EXAMPLE: Only two days till exams start

TRIUMPH / RAGE FACE

A frowning face with steam coming from its nostrils. In Japanese Manga cartoons, this traditionally means 'feeling triumphant', but outside of Japanese culture it's more usually used to represent rage or frustration.

EXAMPLE: The bus was late AGAIN!

LOOK AT THE MESSAGE IN THE BLUE BOX. Choose the best equivalent translation(s) from the orange box. Careful—there could be more than one correct answer! Find out if you got it right on page 172.

Argh not again

a. Argh I can't be ill again!
b. Argh it can't have gone wrong again!
c. Argh I cannot work late again!
d. Argh I hate showering!

WAILING CRYING FACE

A face crying so hard that tears stream from both its eyes. Used to express frustration and unhappiness—often exaggerated for comic effect.

EXAMPLE: They didn't have the shoes in my size

CRYING FACE

A sad face crying a single tear, this emoji is used to express sympathy as well as unhappiness.

EXAMPLE: Just heard your news – I'm so sorry 😢

BLUSHING FACE

With its rosy cheeks and wide eyes, this emoji can be used to show embarrassment, as well as astonishment or shock.

EXAMPLE: I forgot his name in front of everyone. Again. 😳

DISMAYED FACE

Its wide mouth and raised eyebrows give this emoji a look of shock and dismay.

EXAMPLE: I can't believe it!

EMOJIS IN THE DICTIONARY

ARE EMOJIS A BRAND NEW LANGUAGE, or are they a new type of word that's still part of our own language? That's a difficult question to answer.

But what we do know for sure is that 'emoji' has made its way into the English dictionary, and is being used more and more!

In 2002, the word 'emoji' first appeared in the Collins dictionary and between 2014 and 2016 the use of the word 'emoji' quadrupled.

This increased usage of the word 'emoji' is a sign that emojis are making a big impact on the way we communicate... which must mean one thing—emojis are here to stay!

COLD SWEAT FACE

With its concerned expression and cold sweat, this emoji is used to express worry or tension.

EXAMPLE: It's stressing me out so much.

GRIMACING FACE

Its tense expression give this emoji the sense of 'yikes!' or 'eek!'

EXAMPLE: Please don't be angry with me!

SCREAMING FACE

This emoji is crying out in horror—and might remind some people of the famous *Scream* painting by Edvard Munch. But watch out—it can also be used in a positive way to show that someone's hysterically excited.

Scream is a very famous painting and has been celebrated in many ways—including on stamps, as in the picture here.

EXAMPLE: OMG we got front-row tickets!!!

RED ANGRY FACE

This face is red with rage. Used when someone's really furious!

EXAMPLE: That's the final straw!

DIZZY FACE

This face has crosses for eyes on some devices, and dizzy swirls on others. It means someone's bewildered or confused.

EXAMPLE: Too much going on to keep up!

FACE WITH MASK

This face is wearing a mask over its mouth and nose. It's used to talk about illness, but can also mean 'that's disgusting' in a broader sense.

EXAMPLE: The whole family have come down with a horrible bug

ANGRY FACE

A less extreme version of the very similar 'red angry face' emoji.

EXAMPLE: I've had it up to here with this!

SICK FACE

This queasy face looks as though it's about to vomit.

EXAMPLE: You know I hate seafood!

FACE WITH THERMOMETER

A poorly-looking face with a thermometer sticking out of its mouth means someone's not well.

EXAMPLE: Had to call in sick yesterday

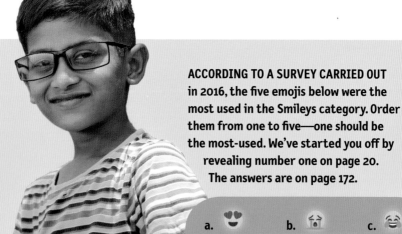

ACCORDING TO A SURVEY CARRIED OUT in 2016, the five emojis below were the most used in the Smileys category. Order them from one to five—one should be the most-used. We've started you off by revealing number one on page 20. The answers are on page 172.

a.   b.   c.   d.   e.

CELEBRITIES USING EMOJIS!

IT IS RUMOURED THAT the pop singer Miley Cyrus has the crying cat emoji tattooed on the inside of her bottom lip.

FACE WITH HALO

This angelically-smiling face with a halo means someone is being well-behaved—or pretending to be!

EXAMPLE: Tidied my room

GEEKY FACE

With its thick-rimmed glasses and buck teeth, this face shows someone's taking a nerdy interest in a subject.

EXAMPLE: Got an A for my homework

SMILING DEVIL

This impish face with horns has a wicked grin. Used to show that someone's up to no good!

EXAMPLE: It's going to be the best party of the year 😈

Thumbs up

Hand gestures

Sit and watch a group of people chatting, and you'll soon notice how much everyone uses their hands as they talk. All around the world, people use gestures to add extra meaning to what they're saying, and to make themselves more clearly understood. (Try sitting on your hands next time you're with your friends, and you'll soon realise how strange and unnatural it feels!)

Things are no different in the world of emojis. There are dozens of hand gestures that you can choose from to make a statement.

All hand-gesture emojis come with bright yellow skin as standard, with the option to choose between four different, more realistic, skin tones.

THUMBS UP

A hand with the thumb pointing up, used to indicate 'Great', 'OK', or 'Well done'.

EXAMPLE: You did a great job today

RAISED HAND WITH FINGERS APART

A palm facing out with the fingers spread apart. This emoji has more than one meaning: the number five, a wave, or to say 'Count me in'.

EXAMPLE: Hi everyone, I'm Alex

PRAYING HANDS

Two hands with palms pressed together. This can either mean 'Thank you' or 'Praying'—for example, for good news.

EXAMPLE: I am the weather's good

WATCH OUT!

Be careful when you're using hand-gesture emojis with friends from around the world! In some cultures, including in the Middle East and parts of West Africa and South America, the thumbs up gesture is considered extremely offensive—the opposite of what it means in Europe and America!

WAVE

A single hand waving, used to mean both 'Hi' and 'Bye'. It can also be used to passive-aggressively chase a response—'Hellloooooo?'

EXAMPLE: See you later!

RAISED HANDS

Two hands raised with palms facing out. Usually used to mean 'Props!' or to hail success.

EXAMPLE: You smashed it!

RAISED FIST

A single clenched fist raised in a sign of victory or power.

EXAMPLE: You've got this

CLAPPING

Two hands clapping, used—either literally or sarcastically—to applaud or praise.

EXAMPLE: Nicely done

BODY LANGUAGE

BODY LANGUAGE can tell us a lot about how a person is feeling, and sets the tone for communication with them.

The arms crossed emoji (right) represents one common body language sign, although interpretations of all body language can vary between different groups of people and cultures.

When a person crosses their arms, it can sometimes be seen a sign they feel defensive or unimpressed! Body language experts, whose job is to analyse and interpret the signs humans give off with their bodies and facial expressions, have on occassion been employed to help actors give a convincing performance, to help leaders project confidently when delivering a speech, or even to help analyse crime scenes.

Sometimes it's vital to limit your body language: the expression 'poker face' refers to successful card players who give their opponents no clues by maintaining a completely neutral facial expression.

While a lot of body language happens subconsciously, emojis with facial expressions and gestures are a fun way of deliberately attaching additional feeling to any message you send.

OK HAND

A hand with finger and thumb forming a circle, signalling 'OK', or 'Everything's good'.

EXAMPLE: Sounds good to me

THUMBS DOWN

A hand with thumb pointing down to indicate displeasure or to cast a 'No' vote.

EXAMPLE: Boo, that's rubbish

HORNS GESTURE

A fist with index and little finger raised to signal 'Rock on'.

EXAMPLE: They said the gig was amazing

RAISED PALM

A hand with palm facing out, fingers together. Used to mean 'Stop', or as a high-five.

EXAMPLE: Stop right there, I've heard enough

EMOJIS FOR EVERYONE

BEFORE 2015, humans in the world of emojis (including all hand gestures) appeared with a pale skin tone.

As emojis took over the world, this lack of different skin tones became more of a problem. People became concerned that emojis didn't represent themselves and their friends.

So, in 2015, new emojis were introduced that allowed people to choose from five different skin colours. What's more, the 'default', or standard skin tone changed—from a pale tone to a bright yellow.

Nobody has bright yellow skin, so now the default skin colour doesn't represent anyone in particular (except the cast of *The Simpsons*!). This means that nobody is left out.

These days, emojis do a much better job of representing the diverse skin colours of people in the world. Can you find an emoji that reflects the colour of your own skin?

VICTORY / PEACE SIGN

Two fingers raised in a V to signal either victory or peace. This emoji has a positive meaning, but a similar gesture with the back of the hand facing forwards is considered very rude in British culture.

EXAMPLE: Fine by me, man

V FOR VICTORY

The V for victory hand gesture was popularised during World War II by the UK Prime Minister, Winston Churchill, and has been used ever since as a symbol of peace. In many countries, it's a popular pose when having your photo taken to show everyone you are feeling happy and positive!

CROSSED FINGERS

With two fingers crossed, this emoji means 'Good luck' or 'I'm rooting for you!'

EXAMPLE: Hope the exam goes well

WHAT DOES THE MESSAGE IN THE BLUE BOX MOST LIKELY MEAN?
Choose from the options in the orange box. The answer is on page 172.

a. Knock on the door at 11 pm.
b. Knock on the door at 2 pm.
c. Knock on the door just once.
d. Knock on the door peacefully.

HOW MANY?!

5

Every day, more than 5 billion emojis are sent around the world... and that's on Facebook's Messenger app alone!

INDEX FINGER POINT

A fist with the index finger pointing up. This emoji has a range of meanings—it can mean someone wants to ask a question, that someone wants people to pay close attention ('Mark my words'), to tell someone off (as if wagging a finger at someone), or just to signal the number one.

EXAMPLE: I've got something to say about that!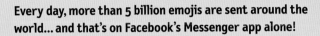

FLEXED ARM

An arm with the bicep muscle flexed, this emoji shows strength or courage.

EXAMPLE: We did it!

HANDSHAKE

Two hands shaking, indicating agreement or welcome.

EXAMPLE: Welcome to the team!

OPEN HANDS

Two hands open. This emoji can be used as 'jazz hands' or to show openness. It can also mean a hug—similar to the 'hugging or jazz hands' smiley.

EXAMPLE: The choice is yours

CALL ME HAND / SHAKA HAND

A fist with the thumb and little finger extended, mimicking a telephone. A similar gesture is also known as the 'shaka'. A traditional Hawaiian sign of friendly greeting, the shaka symbol is a way to say hello or goodbye, thank someone, or show approval and admiration.

EXAMPLE: Call me later?

SELFIE

An arm holding a phone as if taking a selfie.

EXAMPLE: Send me a picture of your new outfit

RIGHT- OR LEFT-FACING FIST

A fist punching to the right (or left), this emoji can be a sign of aggression or endorsement—like a fist bump.

EXAMPLE: Get in!

FIST PUNCH

A clenched fist facing forwards, this emoji can signal either a triumphant 'fist bump' or a more aggressive punch.

EXAMPLE:

Go team

HOW MIGHT YOU REPRESENT THE SENTENCE IN THE BLUE BOX WITH EMOJIS?
Choose the best option from the orange boxes. The answer is on page 172.

Call me at six o'clock. I am so angry!

a.

b.

c.

d.

sassy woman

Humans

Just like real humans, emojis come in all ages, shapes, sizes and colours. Human emojis are often particularly expressive, using not just their faces or their hands to communicate, but their whole bodies—meaning these emojis are great to use if you feel strongly about something!

HEAD MASSAGE

A man or woman having their head gently rubbed. This emoji can refer to anything soothing or calming.

EXAMPLE: I really need a rest

BOW

A person lowering their head in a bow. This emoji can also be used to mean that someone is banging their head on a table in frustration!

EXAMPLE: Whatever you say

RAISED HAND

A man or woman raising their arm, as if to say 'I know!', 'Pick me!', or 'I'm in!'

EXAMPLE: I'll come!

FACEPALM

A man or woman putting their hand over their face—the emoji equivalent of 'Doh!'

EXAMPLE:  I forgot!

MISCOMMUNICATION EMOJI

Most people use to show that someone's feeling bold. But originally, this emoji's hand gesture was meant to be a symbol of help and assistance—hence this emoji's original name, 'information desk person'!

SASSY MAN / WOMAN

A man or woman with one hand extended to the side of their head, as if giving a sassy flip of their hair.

EXAMPLE: Guess who won lead role in the play?

HANDS UP

A man or woman with both hands up by their head and a wide smile—used to show excitement.

EXAMPLE: OMG, amazing news!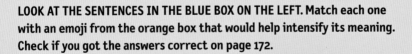

LOOK AT THE SENTENCES IN THE BLUE BOX ON THE LEFT. Match each one with an emoji from the orange box that would help intensify its meaning. Check if you got the answers correct on page 172.

1. I don't care.
2. He styled it quite differently!
3. It's really annoying me.

a.
b.
c.

NO WAY

A man or woman with their arms crossed in front of them as if to say, 'No way!' It can also be a gesture of power, because of its resemblance to the starting pose in some martial arts.

EXAMPLE: Enough is enough

BABY / CHILD / ADULT / OLDER PERSON / WOMAN WITH HEADSCARF

Whatever your age, gender, skin colour or faith, there's an emoji to represent you—these are just a few!

EXAMPLE: You can meet my little brother, and my mum and dad! 👶 👩 👱

WHO KNOWS?

Before the 🤷 emoji was launched, there was the 'Shruggie': ¯_(ツ)_/¯ This symbol was created out of different punctuation symbols and elements of the Japanese alphabet. At one point, the Shruggie was one of the most talked-about symbols on the internet: one man even got it tattooed on his back! Will the introduction of 🤷 kill off the Shruggie? Only time will tell...

54

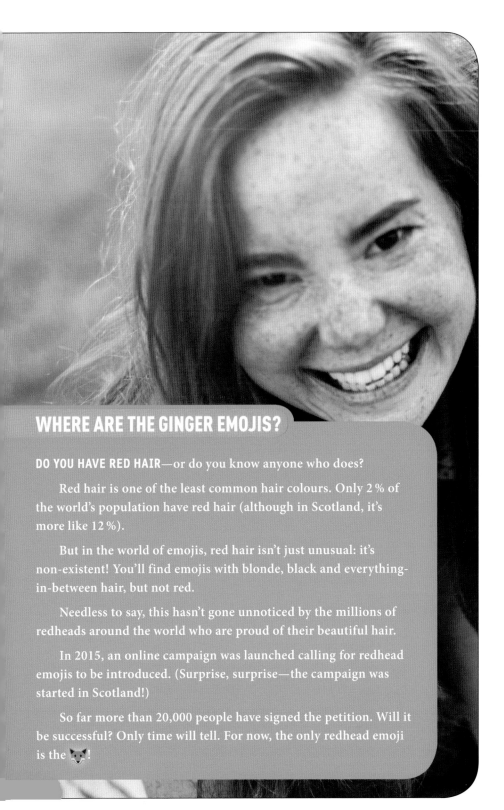

WHERE ARE THE GINGER EMOJIS?

DO YOU HAVE RED HAIR—or do you know anyone who does?

Red hair is one of the least common hair colours. Only 2 % of the world's population have red hair (although in Scotland, it's more like 12 %).

But in the world of emojis, red hair isn't just unusual: it's non-existent! You'll find emojis with blonde, black and everything-in-between hair, but not red.

Needless to say, this hasn't gone unnoticed by the millions of redheads around the world who are proud of their beautiful hair.

In 2015, an online campaign was launched calling for redhead emojis to be introduced. (Surprise, surprise—the campaign was started in Scotland!)

So far more than 20,000 people have signed the petition. Will it be successful? Only time will tell. For now, the only redhead emoji is the 🦊!

scientist

Occupations

On average, someone will spend about one fifth of their waking hours at work over the course of their lifetime. (Phew!) So it's important that we can talk about the kind of work we do, or want to do one day, using emojis.

You won't find every job in the world represented by an emoji, but there are dozens of hard-working emojis that show some of the world's most popular professions.

Every 'professional' emoji comes in a range of options: they can be male or female, and, as with hand gestures and human emojis, you can choose from a selection of skin colours.

TEACHER

A man or woman standing in front of a blackboard with a maths equation on it.

EXAMPLE: Have a great first day back at school!

HEALTH WORKER

A man or woman with a stethoscope. It can refer to a doctor, nurse, pharmacist, other healthcare worker, or simply anyone that cares for someone.

EXAMPLE: What did say?

I'll take good care of you.

POLICE OFFICER

A man or woman in a police uniform, complete with hat.

EXAMPLE: My mum's been a 👮 for 10 years now.

FIREFIGHTER

A man or woman in a firefighter's uniform, complete with helmet. As with the police officer emoji above, it can be used to show that someone is a real-life hero!

EXAMPLE: I always wanted to be a

 She saved the day!

DETECTIVE

A man or woman in a trench coat and dark glasses.
The detective emoji can be used to show that someone is
feeling sneaky—perhaps trying to hunt for gossip!

EXAMPLE:

I found out some great gossip today

Good work – you're so sneaky!

PALACE GUARD

A man or woman in the traditional large furry hat worn by
the guards who protect the Queen at Buckingham Palace.

EXAMPLE:

Have you ever been to London?

CONSTRUCTION WORKER

A man or woman wearing a hard hat for safety. It can be
used to show that someone will fix—or 'sort'—something.

EXAMPLE:

My school is under construction 👷

I've got this. I'll fix it! 👷

PRINCE / PRINCESS

A man or woman wearing a crown, indicating
that someone should be treated like royalty.

EXAMPLE:

Hope you feel like a 🤴 on your birthday!

Good job!

AS YOU MAY ALREADY KNOW, there are lots of different types of jobs that are represented by emojis.

However, what if you're a journalist, or a zookeeper? How do you tell someone what you want to do when there's not a single emoji that reflects your dream job?

The quizzes on this page will show you that all you need to do is be a bit creative in the way you combine your emojis!

LOOK AT THE EMOJI COMBINATIONS IN THE ORANGE BOXES. Match each combination to a job in the blue boxes.

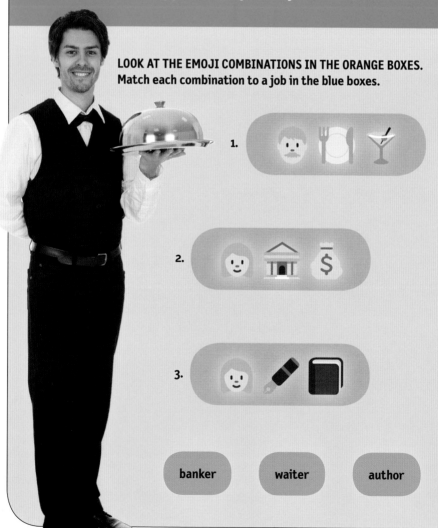

1.

2.

3.

banker   waiter   author

AGAIN, LOOK AT THE EMOJI COMBINATIONS IN THE ORANGE BOXES.
Match each combination to a job in the blue boxes.

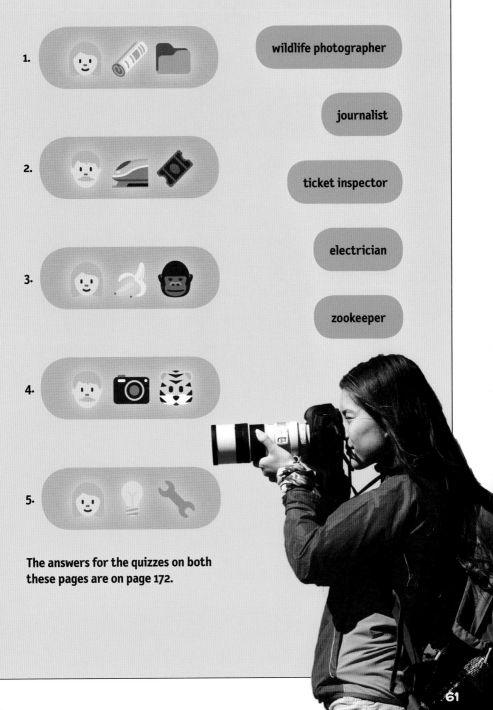

1.

2.

3.

4.

5.

wildlife photographer

journalist

ticket inspector

electrician

zookeeper

The answers for the quizzes on both
these pages are on page 172.

ROCK STAR

The 'singer' emoji on Apple devices, with lightning-shaped face paint and colourful hair, was created in 2016, the year that musician David Bowie died. It was designed as a direct tribute to this flamboyant and groundbreaking rock star.

SCIENTIST

A man or woman wearing protective goggles and a lab coat, holding a beaker of chemicals.

EXAMPLE: He did very well in his chemistry exams

FACTORY WORKER

A man or woman wearing work overalls and a protective visor, holding welding equipment.

EXAMPLE: We had to take the machine back to the factory to be fixed

OFFICE WORKER

A man or woman wearing smart business dress.

EXAMPLE: Dad's got a big meeting tomorrow

ANYTHING YOU CAN DO...

WHAT DO YOU WANT to be when you grow up? 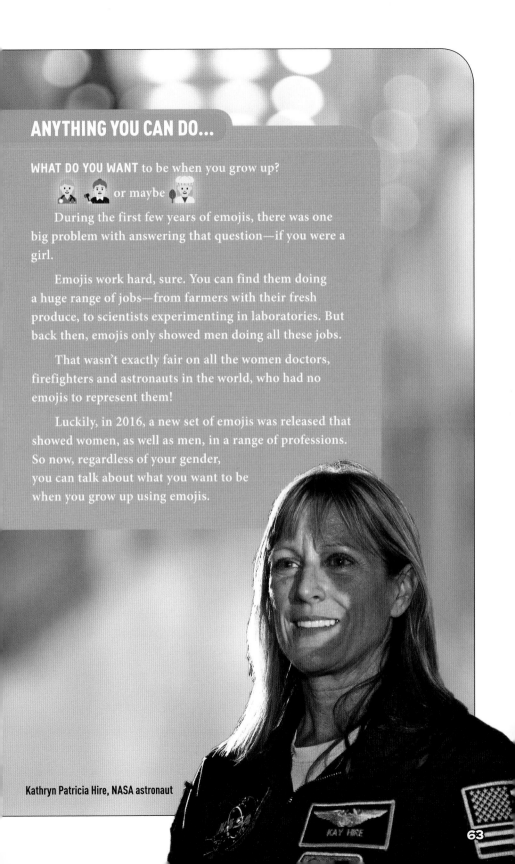 or maybe

During the first few years of emojis, there was one big problem with answering that question—if you were a girl.

Emojis work hard, sure. You can find them doing a huge range of jobs—from farmers with their fresh produce, to scientists experimenting in laboratories. But back then, emojis only showed men doing all these jobs.

That wasn't exactly fair on all the women doctors, firefighters and astronauts in the world, who had no emojis to represent them!

Luckily, in 2016, a new set of emojis was released that showed women, as well as men, in a range of professions. So now, regardless of your gender, you can talk about what you want to be when you grow up using emojis.

Kathryn Patricia Hire, NASA astronaut

MECHANIC

A man or woman wearing work overalls and holding a spanner.

EXAMPLE:

They'll have it repaired in no time

She's handy to have around

CHEF

A man or woman with a wooden spoon and a chef's hat.

EXAMPLE:

Grandma is making a roast dinner for everyone this evening

STUDENT

A man or woman wearing the traditional university dress of black robes and mortarboard hat. Also an emoji to indicate that someone is ready to study.

EXAMPLE:

Happy graduation!

Time for me to study!

FARMER

A man or woman with a straw hat and pitchfork.

EXAMPLE:

We're going to stay with my aunt in the country

MORE THAN ONE

Two *emoji*, or two *emojis*? In Japanese, the endings of words don't change when they're describing more than one thing—so in Japan, the plural is 'emoji', without the 's'. But in English, it's more normal to say 'emojis'.

GENIE

A male or female genie, with blue skin and gold jewellery. It can be used to show that a wish is granted, or that someone is hoping for a wish.

EXAMPLE: Your wish is my command!

FAIRY

A male or female fairy with colourful wings and a green tunic—can show that magic is at work!

EXAMPLE: Just like magic!

THERE ARE SOME MESSAGES ABOUT FANTASY JOBS IN THE BLUE BOX. Match each message with the correct emoji from the orange box.
See if you matched them correctly on page 172.

1. I'm a born swimmer!

2. Keep that garlic away from me!

3. Have you written your list yet?

4. What goes in the potion?

a. 🧛

b. 🧙

c. 🧜

d. 🎅

surfer

Recreations

What do you like to do in your spare time? Most of us have hobbies that we love and which keep us busy, fit, and allow us to express ourselves. Whatever you enjoy—whether it's a sport, martial arts, painting or exploring the countryside on a bike, you'll find an emoji to suit.

—there are so many emojis to express what sport you're doing at the weekend. Here are some of the most common.

SNOWBOARDER

SURFER

SKIER

WEIGHTLIFTER

ROWER

BASKETBALL PLAYER

SWIMMER

MARTIAL ARTS

WRESTLERS

GOLFER

MOUNTAIN BIKER

CYCLIST

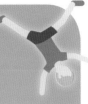

CARTWHEELER

A person doing a cartwheel: this emoji can also show that someone's feeling joyful or excited.

EXAMPLE: Last day of school tomorrow!

RUNNER

A person running—can be used to show the sport, or if someone is in a rush/late for something.

EXAMPLE: Sorry I'm late, I'm on my way!

SPORTS TROPHY

A gold trophy to represent those awarded to winners of tournaments.

EXAMPLE: You're a champ!

SPORTS MEDAL (GOLD, SILVER OR BRONZE)

A medal on a neck-ribbon—this emoji comes in gold, silver or bronze for first, second or third place.

EXAMPLE: So proud of you!

BOXING

A boxing glove: this emoji can also mean that someone's feeling tough, or won't take any nonsense.

EXAMPLE: You show him who's boss

FISHING

A fishing rod with a fish caught on the hook: this emoji can also be used to show that someone has been 'caught' or lured.

EXAMPLE: He swallowed it hook, line and sinker!

BULLSEYE

A bullseye, like the target in a game of darts or in archery, with a dart striking the centre. Can be used to talk about any situation where someone is completely accurate/correct—in the sense of 'hitting the bullseye'.

EXAMPLE: Right on target

JUGGLING

A person juggling three balls in the air. It can also be used to show that someone is very busy and 'juggling' lots of tasks.

EXAMPLE: She could join the circus

LOOK AT THE SPORTING SUPERSTARS IN BLUE
BOXES BELOW. Match each celebrity with the emoji
that represents the sport they are famous for.
The answers are on page 172.

Moeen Ali   Neymar Jr.   Owen Farrell

Maria Sharapova   Rebecca Adlington   Michael Jordan

a.
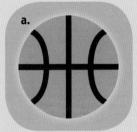

b.

c.

d.

e.

f.

DEUCE!

The Swiss tennis champion, Roger Federer, is one of the
greatest players of all time. He's also one of the world's
biggest champions...of emojis! The star regularly
communicates with his fans by tweeting solely in emojis.

PERFORMING ARTS MASK

The twin masks of comedy (laughing) and tragedy (frowning)—a traditional symbol of the theatre.

EXAMPLE: I'm auditioning for the lead role!

ARTIST'S PALETTE

A palette with a selection of paints. Can be used to show that someone has artistic flair!

EXAMPLE: What did your art teacher say about your work? 🎨

ADMISSION TICKETS

A traditional paper ticket giving entry to a play, film or other event.

EXAMPLE: I've got a spare 🎟 to the show if you want it?

DICE

Dice used in a traditional board game. Also a sign that someone is taking a chance.

EXAMPLE: Oooh, risky! 🎲

HISTORY OF ART

MORE THAN JUST A PRETTY PICTURE... Historians have used paintings and visual art as evidence for understanding how society, customs and attitudes have changed over time. Just as technology has evolved, the quality and composition of painting materials have, too. For example, early paint mixtures often contained natural materials such as calcium or charcoal, while later on, preserving agents allowed painters to work for longer with the paint before it dried, giving them more freedom and control. Some paint textures and colours are especially associated with the era in which they became more widely available, such as a deep red called 'carmine' that's derived from crushed insects, and which is found in some Renaissance paintings.

Other visual clues found in paintings can tell us a lot about people of the past. We can see the types of clothing once favoured by kings, queens and religious figures, and learn what was considered tasteful or beautiful. Wealthy patrons who commissioned portraits often posed with status symbols—for instance, large homes in the background, landscape filled with livestock, or rich fabrics and jewellery. This was a way for them to visually communicate their wealth and status in society.

microphone

Music, communications and technology

Technology is changing and evolving more quickly now than ever before. Things that were cutting-edge a few years before quickly become outdated, and the same is true for emojis! You'll find plenty of emojis that show old-fashioned technology from before the invention of emojis. You'll also spot some that were the latest thing when emojis were brand new, but which seem funny to us now—like pagers, the devices for which emojis were first created. And, of course, you'll find modern inventions like smartphones—the technology that made emojis famous—here, too.

Communication

You might want to show how you're going to communicate a piece of information. Here are some ways to do so with emojis...

RADIO

TELEVISION

CLAPPER BOARD

MOBILE PHONE

TELEPHONE

RECEIVER

PAGER

FILM FRAMES

MEGAPHONE

PAGING THE WAY

Pagers were crucial to the development of the emoji (see page 8), but with the birth of smartphones and other more technologically advanced devices, very few people use a pager nowadays. However, they are still used widely amongst medics. Ambulance pagers can send messages to paramedics that are graded from green (meaning just for the paramedic's information) to red (signalling an emergency that needs urgent attention).

Technology

 —emojis for when you want to talk about a gadget!

DESKTOP COMPUTER

LAPTOP

PRINTER

CAMERA

CAMERA WITH FLASH

VIDEO CAMERA

KEYBOARD

MOUSE

JOYSTICK

VIDEO-GAME CONTROLLER

ELECTRICAL PLUG

BATTERY

If you're a talented musician or a wannabe popstar, some of these musical emojis could come in useful!

MUSICAL STAVE

MUSICAL NOTE

MULTIPLE MUSICAL NOTES

GUITAR

SAXOPHONE

TRUMPET

DRUM

PIANO KEYBOARD

VIOLIN

MICROPHONE

HEADPHONES

STUDIO MICROPHONE

1. Guess the TV series from the emojis below.

2. Guess the film from the emojis below.

3. Guess the song from the emojis below.

The answers to these questions can be found on page 172.

CUSTOM CELEBRITY EMOJIS

In 2015, the American popstar Taylor Swift won the title of 'first custom celebrity emoji'. Twitter users who typed a hashtag related to her *Bad Blood* single would see a relevant emoji appear in their tweet. But, in fact, this wasn't a 'real' emoji. Custom Twitter emojis only work on Twitter's platform, not across all emoji-enabled devices, meaning they aren't part of the standard emoji alphabet.

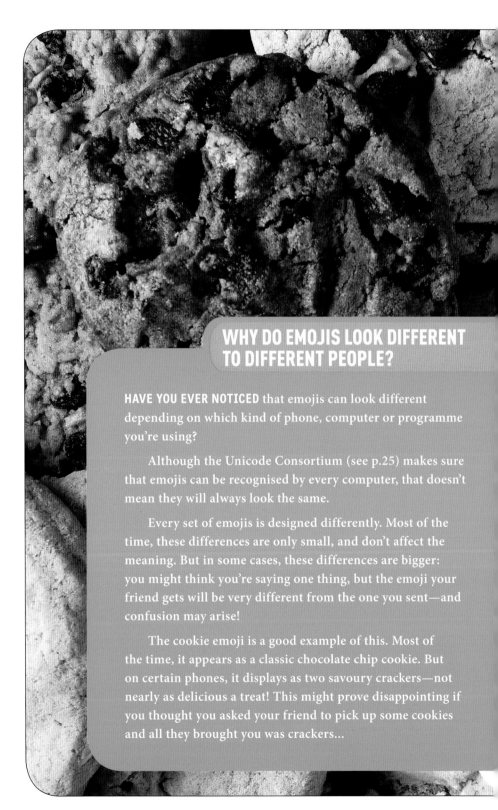

WHY DO EMOJIS LOOK DIFFERENT TO DIFFERENT PEOPLE?

HAVE YOU EVER NOTICED that emojis can look different depending on which kind of phone, computer or programme you're using?

Although the Unicode Consortium (see p.25) makes sure that emojis can be recognised by every computer, that doesn't mean they will always look the same.

Every set of emojis is designed differently. Most of the time, these differences are only small, and don't affect the meaning. But in some cases, these differences are bigger: you might think you're saying one thing, but the emoji your friend gets will be very different from the one you sent—and confusion may arise!

The cookie emoji is a good example of this. Most of the time, it appears as a classic chocolate chip cookie. But on certain phones, it displays as two savoury crackers—not nearly as delicious a treat! This might prove disappointing if you thought you asked your friend to pick up some cookies and all they brought you was crackers...

pizza

Food and drink

'What's for dinner?' must be one of the most frequently asked questions in the world. Most of us love to eat—and we love to talk about what we're eating and drinking, too. There are hundreds of food and drink emojis that represent everything from healthy fresh fruit and vegetables to occasional treats like cake, cookies and cheeseburgers.

CROISSANT

The classic curved flaky breakfast pastry made famous in France (but invented in Austria).

EXAMPLE: Wake up! It's time for

PANCAKES

A pile of thick pancakes with a topping of syrup and butter, as they're typically served in the USA. Like with the croissant emoji above, it can be used to indicate breakfast time.

EXAMPLE: We had such a huge breakfast

FAST FOOD

There are lots of emojis from all over the world for different fast foods—these are just a few!

EXAMPLE: Going to treat myself at lunchtime

KETCHUP OR MUSTARD?

The hotdog emoji was introduced in 2015, after much debate about one very important question... Should it feature ketchup or mustard? In the end, mustard won.

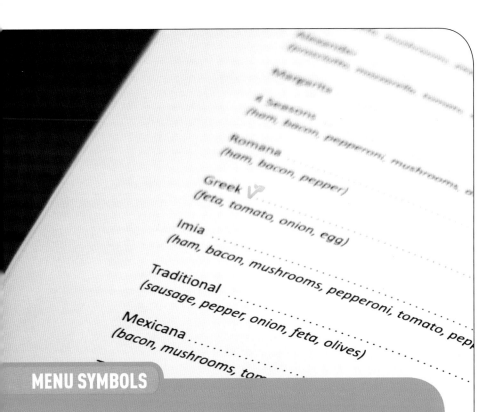

Margarita

4 Seasons
(ham, bacon, pepperoni, mushrooms, o

Romana
(ham, bacon, pepper)

Greek
(feta, tomato, onion, egg)

Imia
(ham, bacon, mushrooms, pepperoni, tomato, pep

Traditional
(sausage, pepper, onion, feta, olives)

Mexicana
(bacon, mushrooms, tom

ili)

MENU SYMBOLS

HAVE YOU EVER NOTICED a green letter 'V' on a menu? This symbol is often used to denote vegetarian or vegan food so that anyone with dietary preferences can quickly scan a menu and see what their options are.

Although the design of the symbols can vary slightly, the green colour and letter 'V' for vegetarian or vegan have long been associated.

Sometimes menus also contain a symbol which shows diners a dish is gluten-free. By including these symbols, not only does it save the diner time when they might otherwise have to read the whole thing, but it means the restaurant can convey the information quickly and clearly without listing all ingredients (although some may choose to do so, too!).

Visual communication is often used to enhance a document filled with words, especially when there are plenty of options!

CHILLI PEPPER

A bright red chilli—the spicy kind! It can be used to show that someone has a fiery temper.

EXAMPLE:

Do you like spicy food?

Don't annoy him – he has a temper!

KIWI FRUIT

Half a kiwi fruit. The kiwi is also associated with New Zealand, after a native species of bird.

EXAMPLE:

I hate kiwi fruit!

RED/GREEN APPLE

A bright shiny apple, this emoji comes in both a red and a green version.

EXAMPLE:

An a day keeps the doctor away!

BRAVOCADO!

In April 2016, the California Avocado Commission launched a petition calling for an avocado emoji. 'Avocado emoji for all!', they demanded. It worked: the avocado emoji was introduced later that year.

COFFEE

A hot cup of coffee, or any other hot drink.

EXAMPLE: My mum can't function until she's had her morning ☕!

CLINKING GLASSES

Two glasses clinking together as if toasting good news or a special occasion.

EXAMPLE: Congratulations!

LOOK AT THE MESSAGES IN THE BLUE BOXES.
Choose an emoji from the orange box that would finish off each message best.
The answers are on page 172.

1. Let's try that new Japanese restaurant.

2. Spag bol? Again? REALLY?!

3. Scrambled or fried?

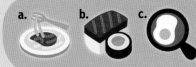
a.   b.   c.

FOOD OFTEN PLAYS a huge part in celebrations and special events right across the world.

From blowing out candles that represent years of age on a birthday cake, to Christmas cakes designed to look like wintery logs, food made for special occasions often contains a lot of meanings and symbols, too!

For example, some people consider dumplings to be a symbol of prosperity because of their likeness to the shape of historic Chinese currency, and because of this, they're often served at Chinese New Year celebrations. Easter eggs symbolise the resurrection of Jesus Christ, and painted ones often reflect the pastel colours and animals that we associate with springtime, when Easter is celebrated.

Food packaging sometimes symbolises what's inside, like beehive-shaped containers of honey, lemon juice inside squeezy lemon-shaped bottles, and the fish-shaped soy sauce bottles which accompany sushi, to show that the sauce goes perfectly with the fish.

IN THE BLUE BOXES, THERE ARE INGREDIENTS FOR SOME WELL-KNOWN DISHES.
Match each set of ingredients to the correct dish from the orange boxes.
The answers are on page 172.

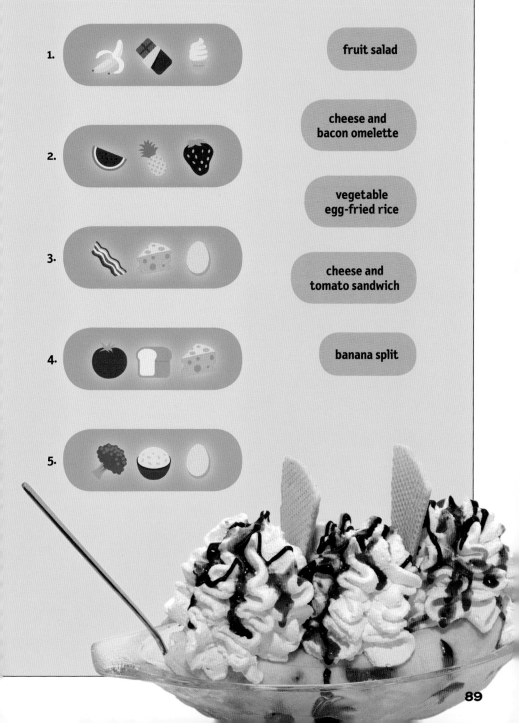

1.

2.

3.

4.

5.

fruit salad

cheese and
bacon omelette

vegetable
egg-fried rice

cheese and
tomato sandwich

banana split

plastic food on display outside
a restaurant in Japan

PLASTIC MENUS

YOU MIGHT HAVE SPOTTED photographs on menus in some restaurants. But in some countries such as Japan, restaurateurs go even further: here, plastic representations of the dishes featured on the menu are a common sight outside restaurants. There are even manufacturers who specialise in creating super-realistic models of dishes such as noodles and soup!

The idea behind these displays is to show potential diners what to expect, as well as to whet their appetite and entice them to come in and taste the real thing after seeing an appealing image.

The models can range from generic dishes to customised speciality dishes for a particular restaurant, and they are often made from moulded plastic before being hand-painted. Similar replica foods are also used on television, and in films and plays as background props.

Visual depictions of food on menus also have another important purpose—they help visiting tourists who are unfamiliar with the language and who might struggle to read a menu understand at a glance what's on offer.

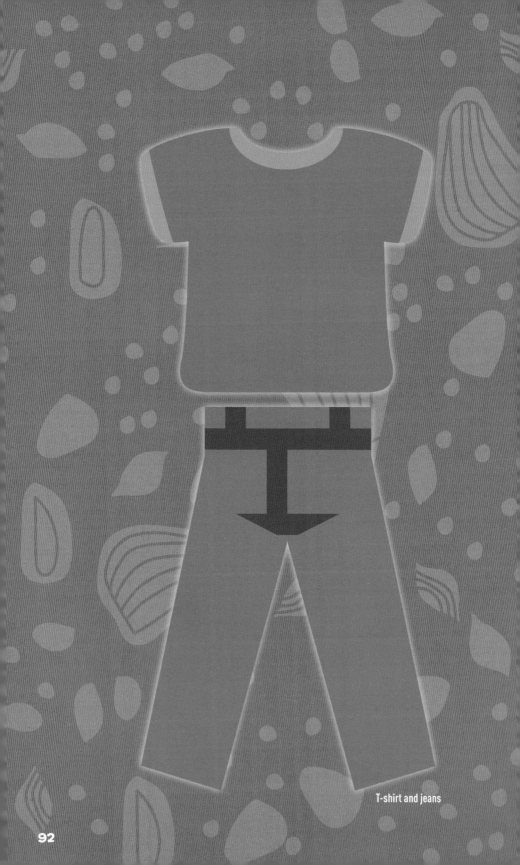

T-shirt and jeans

Clothing

It isn't always easy deciding what to wear. If you need to ask advice, then emojis are here to help! The emojis for clothing and accessories vary hugely from device to device, though, so be careful. You might think you're asking your friend if you should wear your green dress, but he might think you're talking about your blue one!

Clothing

Need to describe what you bought on your last shopping spree? Here are some of the most common clothing emojis.

DRESS

T-SHIRT

KIMONO

JEANS

TIE

TRAINER

SANDAL

BOOT

LEATHER SHOE

DRESSED TO THE NINES

Snapchat puts unique emojis next to celebrities' names in its app to show that their stories come from genuine, 'verified' accounts. They could be anything, from a crown to a cactus. The Canadian actor Shay Mitchell, known for her role in the TV show *Pretty Little Liars*, had her account verified using the 👠.

HOW ARE NEW EMOJIS CHOSEN?

ARE THERE ANY EMOJIS you really wish you could use, but they don't exist? You're not the only one.

From cheese to mermaids, many of today's emojis only came into being because people asked for them, and the Unicode Consortium agreed that they deserve to exist.

What should you do if there's an emoji you want to request? You can go to the Unicode Consortium's website, www.unicode.org, and submit a proposal! That doesn't guarantee that your emoji will be among the new ones released that year, though. The Unicode Consortium considers lots of different factors to decide if a new emoji should be created, including how often it's likely to be used, whether it's too similar to another emoji, whether it's too specific or has too narrow a meaning, or the opposite—if it's too vague.

Some of the most requested emojis include people with curly or afro hair, a cupcake, a disco ball … and a kangaroo! Perhaps they'll find their way onto a screen near you very soon.

COULD YOU BE AN EMOJI TRANSLATOR?

IN THE SUMMER of 2017, Keith Broni woke up to find that he was one of the most talked-about people on the planet. But why?

Keith Broni is a professional emoji translator. When he appeared in a TV news item, people couldn't believe such a job actually existed.

But why not? As you know from this book, emojis can be complicated, and it's all too easy to use them in the wrong way. That's bad enough if you're chatting to friends, but much worse if you're a big company trying to communicate with your customers. Keith Broni helps businesses use emojis correctly, ensures that national differences between the meanings of emojis don't cause confusion from one country to the next, and avoids the mix-ups that can arise from the different appearance of some emojis on different devices (see page 80 for more on this). All in all, a very useful job!

Accessories

—for when words alone can't describe that new crown you have bought...

TOP HAT

GRADUATION HAT

CROWN

BASEBALL CAP

STRAW HAT

DIAMOND RING

UMBRELLA

LIPSTICK

SUNGLASSES

RUCKSACK

HANDBAG

PURSE

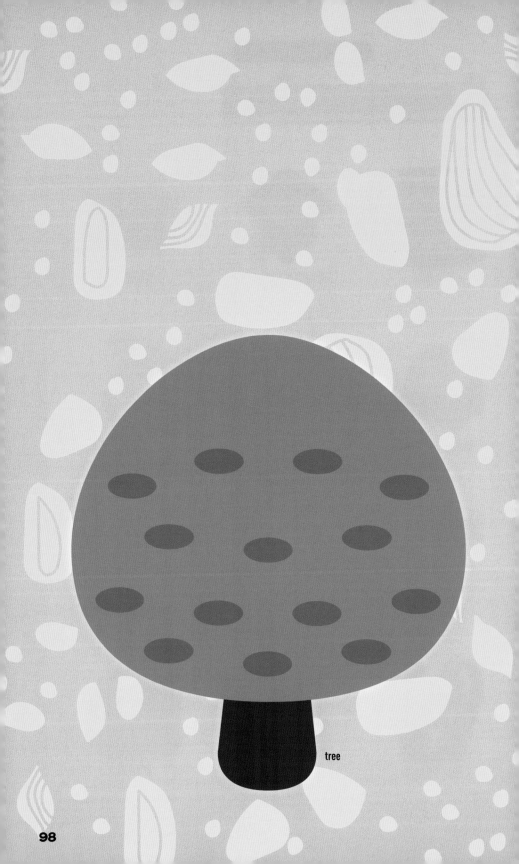

tree

Nature

The natural world is amazingly diverse. Scientists estimate that there are 8.7 million different species of plant and animal—so it isn't surprising that there are more emojis in this category than in any other (not quite 8.7 million, though!).

Emojis that show plants, flowers and creatures often have second meanings as well as the things they literally represent. In every culture around the world, tradition links animals or plants to different emotions, attitudes or behaviours: for instance, in many cultures, a rose means romance, owls indicate wisdom, foxes imply someone or something is cunning, and sharks represent danger—so we might describe someone as a shark as an easy way to say exactly what we think of them.

This rich network of meanings is an important part of our shared culture, and a fun way to use these cute and colourful emojis.

FOUR LEAF CLOVER

A green leaf with four distinct parts, a rare find and a traditional symbol of good luck.

EXAMPLE: Wish me luck!

PALM TREE

A bright green tropical palm—often used to indicate being on a (tropical) beach.

EXAMPLE: The beach looks perfect, so jealous!

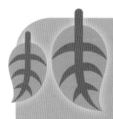

FALLING LEAVES

Autumn leaves falling—a sure sign that the seasons are changing.

EXAMPLE: I love this time of year

LEAVES IN THE WIND

One or two green leaves swirling in the breeze. This emoji can sometimes be used to show that someone is feeling 'breezy' or carefree.

EXAMPLE: It's super windy out there today

GOOD JOB!

The ❀ emoji is very popular in Japanese culture. It can mean 'Well done', and teachers in Japan use a flower stamp very like this emoji to mark especially good work by their students.

CHERRY BLOSSOM

A pink flower that blooms in spring, and a traditional symbol of Japan.

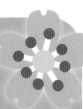

EXAMPLE: The whole street is out in bloom

TULIP

A red or pink tulip—a traditional symbol of the Netherlands and Dutch culture.

EXAMPLE: My dad's family is from Holland

LOOK AT THE EMOJIS IN THE ORANGE BOX. Match each set of emojis to the correct season in the blue box. Check if you got them correct on page 172.

1.

2.

3.

4.

a. spring
b. summer
c. autumn
d. winter

BEAUTY AND THE BEAST

In 2017, the pop singer Ariana Grande delighted her fans by posting a photo of herself in a recording studio with nothing but the emoji as a caption. Why did this make her fans so happy? They knew it was confirmation of rumours that she would be singing on the soundtrack for a new film version of *Beauty and the Beast*—which features a wilting rose very much like the emoji.

SEEDLING

A small green shoot, sometimes shown with the earth it's sprouting from. A sign of hope and new life.

EXAMPLE: Spring is almost here! 🌱

WILTED ROSE

A red rose that's been cut and is wilting with age or neglect, its petals falling. This emoji is often used with feelings of hopelessness, regret and sadness.

EXAMPLE: It didn't work out the way we'd hoped 🥀

HAPPY NEW YEAR!

Ever wondered what the is? This plant is called a kadomatsu, and it is a traditional New Year decoration in Japan. They're placed outside houses to welcome in friendly spirits and bring good fortune for the year ahead.

Know your animals!

You've seen a few plant and flower emojis now, but the next few pages are about animal emojis. See what you already know about animals before reading on with this quiz!

SOME ANIMALS ARE ASSOCIATED WITH PARTICULAR QUALITIES. Look at the sentences in the blue boxes on the left. Match each one to an animal emoji from the orange box that represents it best. The answers are on page 172.

1. I don't know how she wasn't offended by what they said to her!

2. I never really see him these days—he's just always so busy.

3. She's so strong—I can't believe she managed to carry that bag!

4. We've seen a different side to him this week! He's becoming so bold!

a.

b.

c.

d.

DRAGON FACE

A green dragon's face, usually shown with its head turned to the side. This mythical fire-breathing creature is famously fierce and bad-tempered.

EXAMPLE: My new teacher is such a !

T-REX

A large dinosaur with sharp teeth, known to have been a fierce predator. Can be used to describe a fierce person, too.

EXAMPLE: Do you want to watch that movie?

She scares me when she's angry

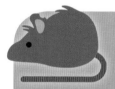

RAT

A grey or white rat with a long pink tail. Rats are considered to be sneaky animals although domestic rats can make friendly pets.

EXAMPLE: Don't on me!

SNAKE

A bright green snake, usually shown coiled, with its forked tongue out.

EXAMPLE: Ooh don't, I'm terrified of 🐍!

SNAKE SYMBOLISM

THE SNAKE EMOJI is sometimes used to suggest deception. Snakes themselves have a long history of symbolism. As well as being part of many myths, legends and rituals in different cultures across the world, snakes have taken on numerous and often very contradictory meanings such as fertility, healing, immortality, good and evil. Here are just a couple of examples.

The ouboros, first seen in Ancient Egypt, is a symbol depicting a snake (or dragon) eating its own tail, forming an infinite loop. As such, it can represent the endless cycle of life and death, or eternity. The ancient Greek symbol, the Rod of Asclepius (named after the god associated with healing and medicine), shows a snake entwined around a staff. Variations of this symbol are still used today by organisations such as the British Medical Association. The much more common association of snakes with deception and evil may originate from the quick movements and venomous bites of some species.

MONKEY FACE (AND VARIATIONS)

A cheeky monkey face that also comes in three variations: with its hands over its eyes ('See no evil'), over its mouth ('Speak no evil') and over its ears ('Hear no evil').

EXAMPLE: My cousin is such a cheeky little 🐵

GIRAFFE

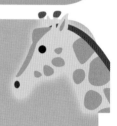

A giraffe's face, either straight on or seen sideways—without showing its famously long neck! Giraffes are known for being extremely tall.

EXAMPLE: I can't believe how tall he is now 🦒

UNICORN HEAD

A colourful unicorn—a famous, mythological, magical animal—complete with horn and colourful mane.

EXAMPLE: It was a magical day! 🦄

LOOK AT THE MESSAGES IN THE ORANGE BOX. They are all missing an emoji (❓). Choose an emoji from the blue box that would fit each message best. The answers are on page 172.

1. Can't believe he remembered my birthday! ❓
2. Listen to what she says—she's not stupid. ❓
3. Calm down—it's not my fault! ❓

a.
b.
c.

GOAT

A grey, white or brown male goat, known as a billygoat, complete with beard and horns. Goats are famously stubborn animals.

EXAMPLE: He's as stubborn as a 🐐

CAMEL

A camel with a single hump. A second camel emoji shows one with two humps.

EXAMPLE: It's the straw that broke the 🐫 back.

RHINOCEROS

A grey rhino, complete with two horns—either just the head, or the whole animal. Rhinos have thick skins and so are a symbol of being tough and resilient.

EXAMPLE: He's so thick-skinned, nothing bothers him 🦏

ELEPHANT

A grey elephant with a long trunk—traditionally, elephants are supposed to have brilliant memories, according to the saying 'an elephant never forgets'.

EXAMPLE: She's got a memory like an

LION FACE

A lion's head with a mane, often used to show bravery or nobility, from the lion's reputation as 'king of the jungle'.

EXAMPLE: You're being so brave

WOLF HEAD

The face of a grey or black wolf—an animal renowned for prowling alone at night.

EXAMPLE: He's a real lone

FOX HEAD

The head of a fox, this emoji can sometimes look very similar to the wolf head emoji. Foxes can symbolise slyness or cunning.

EXAMPLE: There are 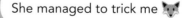 in our neighbourhood.

She managed to trick me

CROCODILE

A green crocodile that varies hugely from device to device. On some it's realistic and frightening, on others it's a cute cartoon croc. Crocodiles are dangerous animals that can capture prey with a single snap of their large jaws. Their 'snappiness' can be representative of a short temper!

EXAMPLE: Don't be so snappy!

CHICKEN

A white chicken—either just the head, or the whole body. Chickens are known for being easily scared.

EXAMPLE: Don't be a

OWL

A brown owl, the traditional symbol of wisdom and learning.

EXAMPLE: My uncle knows everything!

HATCHING CHICK

A happy yellow chick bursting from its shell. This emoji is often used to talk about spring, the season when many baby animals are born, or Easter, the Christian festival which falls in spring.

EXAMPLE: Happy Easter!

EAGLE

Either the head of an eagle, or the bird shown soaring through the sky about to pounce on its prey. The bald eagle is the national emblem of the USA. It also has keen eyesight so that it can spot its next dinner!

EXAMPLE: That's very eagle-eyed of you

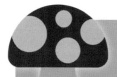

TOADSTOOL

A red-and-white-spotted toadstool. These fungi look pretty, but beware—they're highly poisonous!

EXAMPLE: Don't touch that  Mum says it's really toxic!

CACTUS

A green, spiky cactus. Could be used to show that someone's in a 'prickly' mood!

EXAMPLE: My cousins live way out in the desert

SCORPION

A brown scorpion with its tail raised. The scorpion's curling tale has a poisonous sting at the end, so this creature is associated with unpleasant surprises.

EXAMPLE: That film really had a sting in its tale!

SHARK

A blue or grey shark with sharp teeth. Sharks are fierce predators and are traditionally a symbol of danger.

EXAMPLE: I don't think we should trust him

NATURE SYMBOLISM

THE NATURAL WORLD is full of signs and symbols—if you just know where to look. Naturalists who are experts in animal behaviour know how to interpret signs such as tracks left in the earth or bite marks on trees and plants.

But it's not just animals who communicate visually. We can tell a lot about the natural world by its appearance—for instance, whether things are safe to eat! It's important not to eat anything unless you're 100 % sure what it is. Some people who forage for wild fruit and vegetables determine whether something is safe to eat by the available signs, such as its colour, shape and patterns. For example, many varieties of mushrooms with a red cap are poisonous!

If a food isn't the colour we would normally expect it to be, such as meat that has turned green, this can be a sign it has spoiled and is no longer safe to eat. Size, shape, texture and colour all play a part in how humans—and animals—interpret the natural world.

HUMANS ARE NOT THE ONLY CREATURES who communicate—deliberately or subconsciously—using body language.

The animal kingdom is full of creatures who use their bodies to send messages, from mating dances to signs of aggression.

Time for a belly rub? When dogs roll onto their backs and expose their bellies, they're often showing their owners they trust them and that they're ready to be petted.

In some circumstances, animals bare their teeth as a warning sign to stay away, and this is often accompanied by growling.

Occasionally, animals show off their feathers or fur as part of their mating rituals, such as when male peacocks shake out their beautiful tail feathers to catch the eye of a potential mate.

And it's not just to do with sending signs about mating or aggression—sometimes communication is deceptive. The bioluminescent, glowing lure attached to the face of the anglerfish often attracts smaller fish which then become its dinner. Gulp!

SNAIL

A brown or colourful snail (depending on the device) with its head out of its shell—a famously slow-moving animal.

EXAMPLE: She's coming, but at a pace...

LADYBIRD BEETLE

A bright red beetle with black spots (also called a ladybug). In many cultures, these colourful bugs are considered bringers of good luck.

EXAMPLE: It's bad luck to kill a 🐞

BEE

A bright yellow-and-black-striped bumble bee—the traditional symbol of being busy or hardworking.

EXAMPLE: I've got such a busy day ahead

QUEEN BEE

When the singer and songwriter Beyoncé released a bestselling new album in 2016, two emojis immediately became social media trends: 🐝 (because of Beyoncé's nickname, Queen B), and 🍋 —because her album was titled *Lemonade*.

DOG FACE

A cute puppy with its tongue hanging out.

EXAMPLE: Can I come and play with your new 🐶 soon?

CAT FACE

A cute kitten with whiskers. Cats are said to have nine lives so can sometimes symbolise luck!

EXAMPLE: Your 🐱 is adorable!

He's very lucky to still be alive! 🐱

RABBIT FACE

A grey or white rabbit's face with large front teeth sticking out.

EXAMPLE: I hope the Easter 🐰 brings us lots of chocolate!

FISH

A grey or blue fish—not to be confused with the much more colourful 'tropical fish' emoji.

EXAMPLE: Don't forget to feed the 🐟

Herman Melville

CAN YOU WRITE A BOOK IN EMOJIS?

COULD YOU WRITE A WHOLE BOOK in emojis—with no words at all?
Fred Benenson, a American data engineer, asked himself just that.

He decided writing a book from scratch in emojis might be too
difficult, so he started with an emoji translation of one of the most famous
books in the English language—*Moby Dick* by Herman Melville (published
in 1851). It tells the tale of a whale-hunter who is obsessed with finding
Moby Dick, a whale that had injured him on a previous voyage. At over
200,000 words, it's a long novel—not exactly the easiest choice!

Two years later, thanks to a large team of collaborators, *Emoji Dick* was
published as a real book, with line-by-line translations from English into
emojis. Has anyone ever read it—and enjoyed it? Nobody knows. For now,
it seems like books written with words aren't under too much threat from
emoji literature.

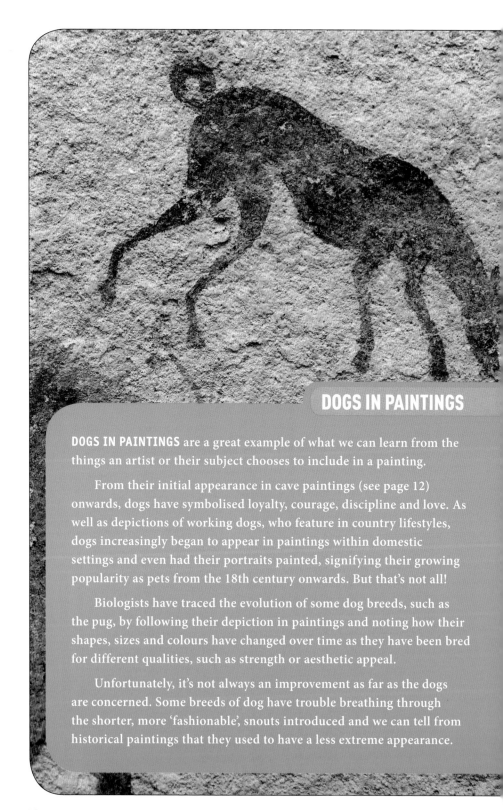

DOGS IN PAINTINGS

DOGS IN PAINTINGS are a great example of what we can learn from the things an artist or their subject chooses to include in a painting.

From their initial appearance in cave paintings (see page 12) onwards, dogs have symbolised loyalty, courage, discipline and love. As well as depictions of working dogs, who feature in country lifestyles, dogs increasingly began to appear in paintings within domestic settings and even had their portraits painted, signifying their growing popularity as pets from the 18th century onwards. But that's not all!

Biologists have traced the evolution of some dog breeds, such as the pug, by following their depiction in paintings and noting how their shapes, sizes and colours have changed over time as they have been bred for different qualities, such as strength or aesthetic appeal.

Unfortunately, it's not always an improvement as far as the dogs are concerned. Some breeds of dog have trouble breathing through the shorter, more 'fashionable', snouts introduced and we can tell from historical paintings that they used to have a less extreme appearance.

EMOJIS FOR ALL DOGS

Did you know? The UK charity Dog's Trust launched a dog emoji keyboard in 2015 with 23 of the most popular breeds including German Shepherd, Yorkshire Terrier, and pug!

COCKEREL

A male chicken—distinguished from female chickens by its red crest and beak. Cockerels greet the dawn by crowing, so are a symbol of early mornings.

EXAMPLE: Wakey wakey, rise and shine! 🐔

DOVE

A white dove holding a branch in its beak. A dove holding an olive branch is the traditional symbol of peace, taken from the story of Noah's Ark in the Old Testament of the Bible.

EXAMPLE: Do you forgive me? 🕊️

THE EMOJIS IN THE ORANGE BOX REPRESENT A FAMOUS BRITISH SAYING.
Do you know what the saying is?

Go to page 172 to see if you were correct.

EWE

A female sheep with woolly white coat, sometimes shown with curling horns. Sheep are famous for following the animals in front of them without thinking.

EXAMPLE: Don't be such a 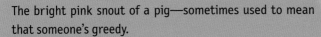—think for yourself!

PIG SNOUT

The bright pink snout of a pig—sometimes used to mean that someone's greedy.

EXAMPLE: How much did you have for dinner?!

MOUSE FACE

A cute cartoon-like mouse face. Mice are famously timid and easily scared.

EXAMPLE: Don't be such a 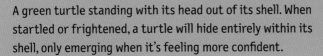, just do it!

TURTLE

A green turtle standing with its head out of its shell. When startled or frightened, a turtle will hide entirely within its shell, only emerging when it's feeling more confident.

EXAMPLE: He's really started to come out of his shell this year

THE THREE WISE MONKEYS

THE MONKEY FACE EMOJIS,  are some of the cutest emojis of all. But have you ever wondered why there are so many different monkey expressions to choose between—more than any other emoji animal?

Three monkeys—one with its hands over its eyes, one with its hands over its mouth, and one covering its ears—are traditional characters in Japanese culture. They are known as sanzaru, or 'the three wise monkeys', and date back to the 17th century or earlier.

In Japan, they represent different elements of wise behaviour: the wisdom of being careful about what you look at, listen to, or say. However, in many other countries, they are used differently. You'll often see these emojis used in English-speaking countries with the sense of 'not wanting to look', 'trying not to laugh' or 'pretending not to listen'— very different from their wise origins!

globe

Geography and transport

Since emojis have taken over the world, it's only fair that you can use them to describe your world, too!

Whether you're talking about natural landmarks, your town or city, or how you're getting from A to B, you'll find all the emojis you could need to explore, plan an adventure, or daydream about a holiday. Where will emojis take you next? It's time to find out...

GLOBE

This emoji of planet Earth comes in three variations, each looking at the globe from a different angle, to show different continents.

EXAMPLE: We have to fly to the other side of the  to see them.

SNOW-CAPPED MOUNTAIN

A range of mountains capped with snow. Another similar emoji shows Mount Fuji, the highest peak in Japan.

EXAMPLE: You can see the  in the distance.

STATUE OF LIBERTY

The face of the Statue of Liberty, which stands on the shore in New York. It is a symbol of freedom.

EXAMPLE: My big brother has moved to NYC

MAPPING JAPAN

Japan is the only country in the world to have its own map emoji.

ARE EMOJIS ART?

ARE EMOJIS WORKS OF ART?

It's almost impossible to define exactly what art is, and the definition changes over time—which makes this a very hard question to answer.

But what we do know is that curators from New York's prestigious Museum of Modern Art (MoMA), where you can find works by great artists such as Salvador Dalí, Frida Kahlo and Jackson Pollock, think the answer is 'Yes'!

In 2016, the first-ever set of 176 emojis, created by Shigetaka Kurita in 1999, became part of the museum's permanent collection. As MoMA explained, 'Shigetaka Kurita's emoji are powerful manifestations of the capacity of design to alter human behaviour'. Or to put it another way… emojis have changed our lives forever, which makes them too important to ignore!

Of course, we use them here in this book, too—and in social media as a language/code as well. Can something be both art *and* language? What do you think?

CO-ORDINATING TRAFFIC

TRAFFIC CO-ORDINATORS ASSIST in guiding traffic, sometimes for special events where there are more vehicles than usual, by holding traffic signs, wearing brightly coloured gloves, and sporting hi-visibility vests that ensure they're seen easily. This helps ensure their own protection while they're working on or beside roads, as well as drawing drivers' attention to their signals.

In the 1990s, Antanas Mockus, the Mayor of Bogota, Colombia, tried an unusual approach to reduce public offences in the city. Aware of how important visual demonstration could be, he hired a group of mimes to follow and mimic citizens who carried out offences such as jaywalking. He followed this with an even bigger spectacle, hiring over 400 mimes to become traffic co-ordinators.

The sight of the mimes on street corners drew attention to the problem of traffic congestion and reckless driving, and the experiment has since been repeated elsewhere.

Transport

Need your friend to cycle over quickly? Got to jump on a train straightaway? These transport emojis might just come in handy!

TRAIN

TAXI

CAR

SCOOTER

BICYCLE

BUS

MOTORBIKE

MOPED

METRO / SUBWAY

AEROPLANE

HELICOPTER

ROCKET

FINNISH LADYBIRDS

The seven-spot ladybird is Finland's national insect, one of the country's seven natural symbols, as decided by the public! The bright red colour of ladybirds warns predators that they're not tasty to eat.

UNTRANSLATABLE WORDS

EMOJIS ARE DESIGNED to be universally recognisable symbols, but occasionally, special sets of pictograms (simple images representing something—just like emojis) are created. Finland was the first country in the world to create its own pictograms representing Finnish customs, words, and emotions! These include the joulutorttu, which is a windmill-shaped Finnish pastry with plum jam in the middle; flag-waving faces of hope and despair for watching Finland's entries in the Eurovision Song Contest; and another to depict Finland beating its closest neighbour and biggest rival, Sweden, in sports competitions!

There are also some words that are particular to one country's culture that don't have a straightforward one-word translation into other languages. Among Finland's emoji set is kaamos, which means the feeling of sunless days, reflecting their long, dark winters.

Here are some other 'untranslatable' words:

komorebi: this Japanese word means the light which filters through trees

saudade: from Portuguese, this is a bittersweet feeling of longing for something which is long gone

jayus: an Indonesian word which means a joke that is funny precisely because it is so bad

What might an emoji or pictogram for these look like?

AIRCRAFT LANDING SIGNS

AEROPLANES AND HELICOPTERS rely on sophisticated technology to navigate the skies, with cockpits full of buttons and dials that feed information back to control rooms. But like other forms of transport, they also use visual communication, and there are some signs that you can spot, too!

Just as lighthouses have a beam of light to signal cliffs to nearby ships, buildings that are very tall often have red lights on top to mark them out to aircraft. And, if you look into the sky at night, you might see the lights on planes themselves, which help prevent accidental collisions between planes.

Lights are also used on airport runways to help aircraft land safely and carefully, and can show staff on the ground when it's safe to approach.

Helipads use a big letter H as a symbol to show helicopter pilots where to safely land. These can be found in a variety of places—some quite surprising—from the tops of buildings to the back of ships!

Where in the world...?

Countries around the world have their own traditions which can come in the form of food, music, dance, theatre—the list is endless!

LOOK AT THE EMOJI MESSAGES IN THE BLUE BOXES. Each set of emojis represents a country. Match each message to a country in an orange box. Have a look at page 172 to see if you matched them correctly.

1.

Italy

France

2.

USA

Japan

3.

China

4.

5.

131

chequered flag

Flags

People have used flags to communicate without words for thousands of years. So it's only natural that they feature in the world of emojis, too.

Flags are best known for representing different countries—so, as you'd expect, there are dozens and dozens of flag emojis. No matter what nation you come from, you're almost certain to find your flag in emoji form. But flags are also a powerful symbol of belonging to other kinds of communities, not just nations—and some of those, such as the gay community, are proudly represented by emoji flags too.

Who will you fly the flag for?

ALMOST EVERY NATION in the world has an emoji flag to represent it, just as every nation has its own flag.

Three of the four separate nations of the United Kingdom have their own distinct flags. However, they weren't represented by flag emojis until October 2017, when Scottish, English and Welsh flags were included in the latest update:

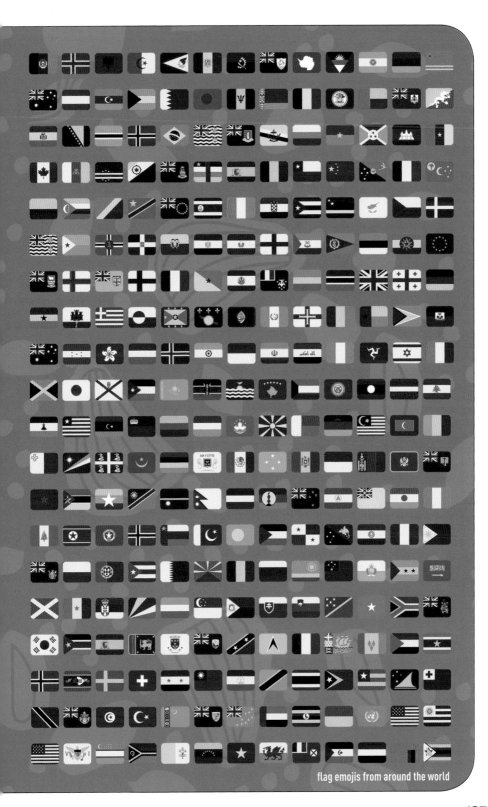

flag emojis from around the world

VEXILLOGRAPHY

AS YOU CAN SEE from the emojis, flags are varied in their design, with all kinds of patterns, symbols and colours on display.

We know that flags are carefully designed to represent their countries, but how? The art of designing flags is called vexillography, and vexillographers have a lot to consider when they are designing a flag for a country or an organisation.

Like any other sign or symbol, the design of flags includes practical considerations, such as how a flag will look when it is flying on a pole, whether a flag will be easily recognisable at different sizes, and how it stands out from other flags.

As for design, let's take the United Kingdom's flag, created in 1801, as an example. The red, white and blue design actually takes three existing flags and combines them—the white saltire of St Andrew, the red cross of St George, and the red saltire of St Patrick. These represent nations within the United Kingdom.

Other countries' flags may represent constituent states, such as the fifty stars that represent the USA's fifty states on its flag. Flags usually only change when a country changes its government or regime in dramatic ways, or when a country splits into separate independent nations. In 2016, New Zealand held a referendum on its flag, but after two rounds of voting, it was decided to keep the existing flag, which shows a pattern of stars representing the constellation of Crux, the Southern Cross.

Flags represent their countries, but the symbolism within their design is just as interesting.

windsock indicating wind direction

SEMAPHORE

SEMAPHORE IS THE PRACTICE OF COMMUNICATING using flags or sticks by waving and holding them in specific patterns. This method of communicating information over distances uses a recognised code, in which each letter in the alphabet is assigned a position.

Semaphore has been used since the 19th century, well before radio was available at sea or in other situations where people needed to communicate across open water or country. Today, semaphore still exists and is sometimes used in emergencies, when other forms of communication are unavailable or have failed, or in low light, using lighted sticks instead of flags.

There is a long tradition of using flags and symbols to communicate at sea, and semaphore is just one way in which flags can be used to send important messages. Another common method of visual communication at sea is to use flags or windsocks to determine wind direction, or to signal dangerous high winds and warn bathers to avoid swimming.

While some territories have local interpretations of what flags mean, there are various internationally agreed standards, which make a visual language like semaphore both practical and effective on the ocean waters.

SOS in semaphore—SOS is the international signal showing that someone is in distress

CHEQUERED FLAG

This black and white flag is waved to start a motor race—it means 'Go!'

EXAMPLE: On your marks, get set...

RAINBOW FLAG

This flag is known as the lesbian, gay, bisexual and transgender (LGBT) flag. It is often seen flying during 'Pride' events, which celebrate gay rights and LGBT movements.

EXAMPLE: There's a Pride parade tomorrow

BLACK FLAG

A black flag flying in the wind. Black flags are flown in times of mourning.

EXAMPLE: Sad news

WHITE FLAG

A white flag flying in the wind. Flying a white flag is a sign of surrender in warfare.

EXAMPLE: Ok, I give in. You win!

JOLLY RODGER

THE 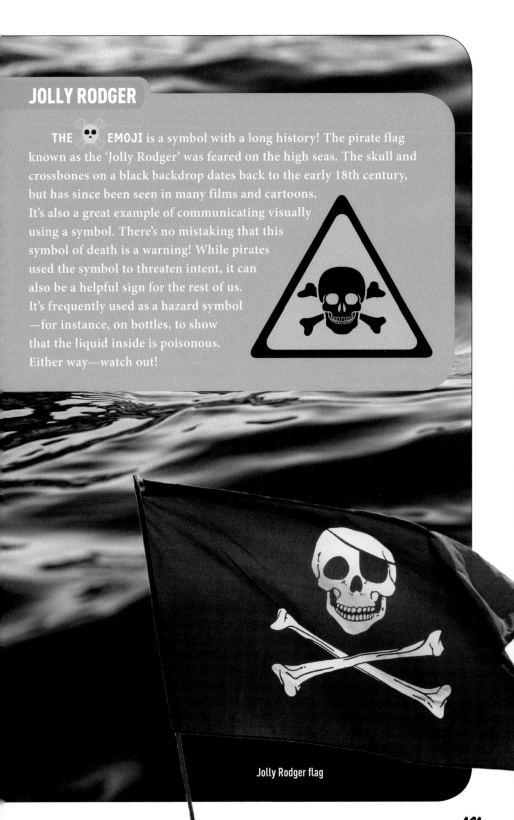 EMOJI is a symbol with a long history! The pirate flag known as the 'Jolly Rodger' was feared on the high seas. The skull and crossbones on a black backdrop dates back to the early 18th century, but has since been seen in many films and cartoons. It's also a great example of communicating visually using a symbol. There's no mistaking that this symbol of death is a warning! While pirates used the symbol to threaten intent, it can also be a helpful sign for the rest of us. It's frequently used as a hazard symbol —for instance, on bottles, to show that the liquid inside is poisonous. Either way—watch out!

Jolly Rodger flag

moon with face

Time, weather and occasions

Got something to celebrate? There's an emoji for that.

Whether you want to wish someone a happy birthday, Christmas, New Year or Hannukah, emojis are the perfect way to mark a special day, at any time of the year, no matter the season or the weather. So it's lucky that winter snow, summer sunshine and everything in between all find their place in the world of emojis as well.

And, just as these milestones mark the passing of time, you can use emojis to do that, too. So don't delay—what are you waiting for?

WHAT'S THE TIME, MR WOLF?

The clock emojis, showing a range of different times, are some of the least-used emojis in the world. After all, it's much easier to type the time than to expect your friend to read a tiny picture of a clockface!

ALARM CLOCK

An alarm clock, with two bells on the top which a beater strikes to make a loud, ringing noise. Alarm clocks remind people to wake up at a certain time in the morning, so are used as a symbol to mean 'Remember!'

EXAMPLE: Remember you have an early start tomorrow! 🕐

HOURGLASS WITH FLOWING SAND

A traditional hourglass, used to measure periods of time as the sand trickles from top to bottom. Because it is so easy to see the sand slipping away, the hourglass is a symbol of time passing or slipping away. It can also be used to show that someone is waiting (patiently or impatiently!).

EXAMPLE: The holidays are passing so quickly

SIGN OF THE TIMES

Eagle-eyed Apple users might spot that the watch emoji looks slightly different to them than to others. That's because Apple changed it when they released the Apple watch, to show off their latest invention.

NEW MOON

A dark moon, as appears every 28 days in the lunar cycle. When the moon is new, it is barely visible in the night sky.

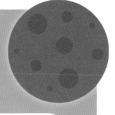

EXAMPLE: It's pitch black outside tonight

FULL MOON

A full moon, as appears every 28 days in the lunar cycle.

EXAMPLE: The  looks amazing tonight.

SUN WITH FACE

A smiling yellow sun. It can also be a symbol for joy and happiness.

EXAMPLE: Yay, the sun has come out!

THERMOMETER

A thermometer with red liquid inside it, used to measure either the air temperature or a person's body temperature, to see if they are unwell.

EXAMPLE: It's so hot outside!

Weather

For some people, talking about the weather is a hobby! Here are some ways to express what the weather is like with emojis.

SNOWFLAKE

SNOWMAN

SNOW CLOUD

CLOUD WITH SUN

CLOUD WITH SUN AND RAIN

THUNDERSTORM

TORNADO

WIND

FOG

RAIN CLOUD

SUN

RAINBOW

JACK O'LANTERN

An orange pumpkin with a spooky face carved into it, as is traditional at Halloween.

EXAMPLE: Happy Halloween!

FIREWORKS

Brightly coloured fireworks exploding in a night sky. This emoji can also symbolise that someone is 'exploding' with excitement or is very passionate about something.

EXAMPLE: Did you go to see the ?

She was exploding with excitement! 🎆

WRAPPED GIFT

A neatly wrapped present with colourful wrapping paper and a pretty bow, symbolising celebrations.

EXAMPLE: I have to go Christmas shopping 🎁

BALLOON

A red balloon floating with its string. This could also mean that someone feels like they've got rid of a 'weight off their shoulders' and feels a lot 'lighter'.

EXAMPLE: Can you help us decorate for his party?

HOW ARE YOU CELEBRATING on 17th July?

If you're not sure what there is to celebrate, then you need to make a note in your diary right now—because 17th July is World Emoji Day!

Since 2014, emoji fans around the world have celebrated their favourite way to communicate with parties, awards and events. The celebrations centre on New York, where the Empire State Building is lit up in yellow, and the winners of the World Emoji Awards are announced from the city's Stock Exchange. (Categories include 'Best New Emoji', 'Most Anticipated Emoji' and 'Lifetime Achievement Award'.)

But why 17th July?

The founder of World Emoji Day, Jeremy Burge, chose this date because it's displayed on the calendar emoji for Apple users. Naturally!

Let's celebrate!

People celebrate different events around the world, but many celebrations have similar themes wherever they're celebrated.

LOOK AT THE EMOJI MESSAGES IN THE BLUE BOXES. Match each emoji message to the event in the orange box it relates to. The answers are on page 172.

1.

Chinese New Year

2.

Valentine's Day

Bonfire Night

3.

Christmas

4.

Easter

5.

No entry sign

150

Symbols

A symbol is a simplified image or mark that's easy to recognise and which carries a specific meaning—all without needing to use words or language. If you think that sounds a lot like a description of emojis, you'd be right! Emojis are a kind of symbol.

But there are also emojis that represent existing symbols from different groups or systems of symbols across the world. (Yup, that's right—symbols... of symbols.) You'll find emojis that feature roadside and traffic symbols next to symbols that are thousands of years old, like the signs of the zodiac. Then there are the symbols that are so common that we don't even stop to think about them in daily life, like a tick to mean 'correct', or a cross to mean 'wrong'. Once you've explored the world of emoji symbols, keep a look out for all the different symbols you use to 'read' your world, without even thinking about it, as you go through your day—you'll be amazed how many there are!

Give me a sign!

There are lots of signs and symbols that we use every day, but did you know that many of them also have emoji forms?

LOOK AT THE EMOJIS IN THE BLUE BOXES.
Match each one to its meaning in the orange box. The answers are on page 172.

1.

2. WC

3. ATM

4.

5.

6.

a. Cash machine

b. Warning!

c. No cycling

d. No phones

e. Radioactive material

f. Toilets

WARNING

A yellow triangle with a black exclamation mark in the centre.

EXAMPLE: Don't go in there!

EXCLAMATION MARK

A single red exclamation mark which can mean 'Beware!' A double version and a '?!' version also exist.

EXAMPLE: Watch out !

100 POINTS

An underscored '100' that looks like it's been handwritten, this emoji is supposed to represent a test score (as marked by a teacher), but is more often used to indicate enthusiasm—100%!

EXAMPLE: Couldn't agree more 100

HOW MUCH?!

Want to see exactly what emojis are being used when, and how often they've been used? Just visit www.emojitracker.com, which keeps track of every emoji used on Twitter—in real time!

SOS

A red square with SOS on it—as if a button. SOS is the international signal of distress in Morse code, a form of communication invented in the mid-19th century.

EXAMPLE: Help! I'm stuck talking to them

TICK

A thick black tick or check mark—meaning a task is finished or completed.

EXAMPLE: All done ✔

CROSS

A heavy red cross, often used to show negativity or refusal—'No' or 'Wrong answer!'

EXAMPLE: No way! ✗

STOP SIGN

A red octagon, used as the traffic symbol for 'Stop' in many countries.

EXAMPLE:  right there

ANIMATED EMOJIS

THE EMOJIS THAT WE KNOW and love are static images. They don't move on our screens. But there's no reason why that has to be the case.

In fact, animated versions have existed from the very earliest days of emojis in Japan, and were one of the main ways that phone manufacturers would try to outdo each other in the battle to win customers.

However, Apple's decision to use only static emojis when it introduced them to the iPhone meant that as emojis spread around the world, it was these static versions that became the norm.

In 2017, Apple announced that it would be introducing what it calls 'Animojis' into our lives. Instead of the simple animations of classic emojis that have existed for many years, these new creations will allow users to animate emojis using their voice and own movements, by linking them to their phone cameras. Ever wanted to make the monkey, fox, alien, chicken, or even smiling pile of poo move and sound like you? Thanks to Animoji, you can.

NO ENTRY

A red circle with a white rectangle in the centre, used to mean 'No entry' on roads and other places in many countries.

EXAMPLE: They're not coming in

PEACE

The worldwide symbol for peace, invented in the 1950s as the logo for the British Campaign for Nuclear Disarmament (CND), it is often used in protests and on peace marches.

EXAMPLE: Chill out 🕊

ZODIAC (VARIOUS)

The traditional sign for Aries, the first of the twelve signs of the zodiac used in astrology (a system of thought which believes that the arrangement of the stars and planets influences what happens to people). All twelve signs of the zodiac have their own emoji.

EXAMPLE: Happy birthday!

TM

TM

The international sign of a 'trademark'—a symbol, word or phrase registered by a company so that nobody else can use it.

EXAMPLE: It was my idea! **TM**

heart

Friendship and dating

When you feel really strongly about someone, there's only one way to show them how much you care.

Forget flowers or chocolates—say it with emojis!

Staying in touch with your loved ones is the most common reason that people all over the world use emojis. So it's no surprise there are plenty of ways to express your feelings towards friends, family or partners—and a few to turn to if you're ever broken-hearted, too...

HEART

A red heart (not to be confused with the 'heart suit' emoji, which is part of a set of four emojis from a deck of playing cards). Used to mean 'love'.

EXAMPLE: Thank you

BROKEN HEART

A red heart broken in two, representing heartbreak and sorrow.

EXAMPLE: I can't believe it

HEART WITH ARROW

A pink heart pierced by an arrow, as if by one of Cupid's arrows. In Roman mythology, the god Cupid would shoot unsuspecting people with his bow and arrow, causing them to fall in love.

EXAMPLE: She's really into him

HEAVY HEART

A red heart with a circle underneath. This emoji technically represents 'a heavy heart'—that is, sadness—but is often used as an alternative to other heart emojis for variety, or as a kind of exclamation, because it resembles an exclamation mark.

EXAMPLE: He's so cute!

GROWING HEART

A pink heart that looks as though it's swelling to become more and more full of love.

EXAMPLE: I just love him soooo much 💗

THERE ARE LOTS OF DIFFERENT COLOURED HEARTS IN THE EMOJI ALPHABET— and they can have a range of meanings. Have a look at the coloured hearts in the orange box. Decide what each heart might represent from the blue box. You will find the answers on page 172.

a. jealousy   b. happiness   c. sorrow   d. peace

1.

2.

3.

4.

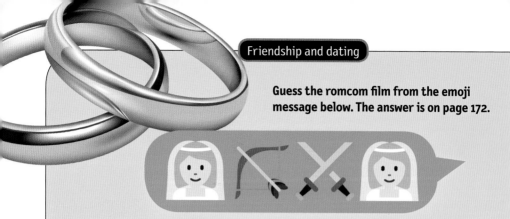

Guess the romcom film from the emoji message below. The answer is on page 172.

MAN IN TUX

A man in a dinner jacket and bow tie, often used to mean 'groom' when used in partnership with the 'bride' (see below), but also that it's time to dress up in your best outfit!

EXAMPLE: Let's see the wedding photos!

BRIDE

A woman in a white veil, as if in traditional Western wedding dress.

EXAMPLE: Her wedding dress was beautiful!

WILL YOU MARRY ME?

In 2015, just after World Emoji Day, Pepsi released an advert showing a man proposing to his girlfriend... using special Pepsi emojis! (She said yes.)

EMOJI COMBINATIONS

Some emojis aren't actually single emojis at all. They're made by combining sequences of multiple emojis. For instance, the emoji is actually 🧑, 💚, 💋 and 🧑 emojis combined. You might notice this sometimes if you use an emoji on a device where the combination isn't supported: it will appear broken down into its individual parts.

PEOPLE HOLDING HANDS

A couple holding hands: either a man and a woman, two men, or two women. Can represent a romantic relationship or friendship/partnership.

EXAMPLE: They make such a cute couple 👭

FAMILY SET

No two families are alike, which is why there are so many variations on the family emoji: from one mum or one dad, to a mum and dad, to two mums or two dads, all with different combinations of children.

EXAMPLE: Are you going with your parents?

PEOPLE KISSING

Two people kissing: either a man and a woman or two men and two women. This can mean a romantic kiss or just a friendly one.

EXAMPLE: You're the best 💏

COUPLE WITH HEART

Like the 'people kissing' emoji on page 163, this emoji comes in different combinations. And again, it can be used to show romantic love or simply love between friends.

EXAMPLE: They get on so well

PREGNANT LADY

A woman with a baby bump—showing that someone is expecting the imminent arrival of a new baby.

EXAMPLE: When's the baby due?

LOOK AT THE MESSAGES IN THE ORANGE BOX. They are all missing an emoji (**?**). Choose an emoji from the blue box that would fit each message best. The answers are on page 172.

1. I don't even know why she left... **?**

2. He looked so handsome on his wedding day! **?**

3. I love her more each day **?**

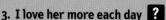

a.   b. ♥   c.

EMOJI POETRY

THROUGHOUT THE CENTURIES, people have turned to poetry to express their deepest feelings—of love, sorrow, wonder or joy. Now, emojis have given a new generation of poets even more ways to be creative.

The respected literary journal *The Paris Review* has published emoji translations of classic poetry, challenging its readers to identify them. Meanwhile, some writers, including the American poet Stephanie Berger, have taken to crafting their own poems in emojis as well as in words. Berger has even published a short collection of emoji poetry. And why not? Poets have always experimented with language to find new, unusual and powerful ways to communicate. Emojis are another way to do just that.

nerdy face

Test your emoji knowledge

By now, you're probably fluent in emoji! Look at the following quiz pages to see how much you've learnt.

eMoji Quiz

NOW YOU'RE FLUENT IN EMOJI, it's time to put your knowledge to the test!

Here are some popular songs or films translated into emojis. Sometimes they explain the plot or story, sometimes the emojis stand in for words in the titles.

How many can you decode? Once you think you've cracked them all, check page 172 for the answers. To help you out, there's an emoji next to each clue to show you whether it's a film (▦) or song (🎤).

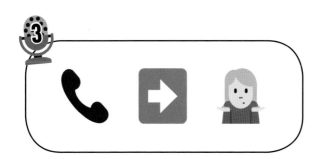

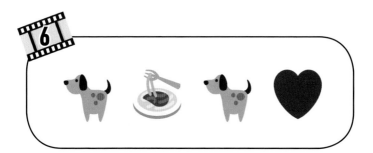

16

17

18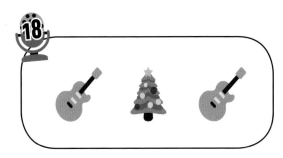

19

20

21

AnSWeRS

Page 21
1. d
2. a
3. b
4. e
5. c

Page 23
1. c   2. a   3. b

Page 27
b

Page 31
a, b, c

Page 36
1. c
2. a
3. b
4. e
5. d

Page 46
c

Page 49
c

Page 53
1. c   2. a   3. b

Page 60
1. waiter
2. banker
3. author

Page 61
1. journalist
2. ticket inspector
3. zookeeper
4. wildlife photographer
5. electrician

Page 65
1. c   3. d
2. a   4. b

Page 71
a. Michael Jordan
b. Owen Farrell
c. Rebecca Adlington
d. Maria Sharapova
e. Moeen Ali
f. Neymar Jr.

Page 79
1. *Paw Patrol*
2. *Brave*
3. *Dancing In The Moonlight*

Page 87
1. b   2. a   3. c

Page 89
1. banana split
2. fruit salad
3. cheese and bacon omelette
4. cheese and tomato sandwich
5. vegetable egg-fried rice

Page 101
1. c
2. d
3. a
4. b

Page 103
1. c   3. d
2. b   4. a

Page 106
1. a   2. c   3. b

Page 118
It's raining cats and dogs.

Page 131
1. France
2. Italy
3. China
4. Japan
5. USA

Page 149
1. Chinese New Year
2. Bonfire Night
3. Christmas
4. Valentine's Day
5. Easter

Page 152
1. d   4. e
2. f   5. c
3. a   6. b

Page 161
1. c
2. a
3. b
4. d

Page 162
Bride Wars

Page 164
1. c   2. a   3. b

Emoji quiz (pages 168-171)
1. *Hit Me Baby One More Time*
2. *The Lion, The Witch and The Wardrobe*
3. *Call Me Maybe*
4. *Titanic*
5. *Cinderella*
6. *The Lady and The Tramp*
7. *Jurassic Park*
8. *Chicken Run*
9. *Finding Nemo*
10. *The Sound of Music*
11. *Batman*
12. *The Lion King*
13. *Jaws*
14. *Alien*
15. *Up*
16. *Dancing Queen*
17. *American Pie*
18. *Rocking Around the Christmas Tree*
19. *Umbrella*
20. *Set Fire to the Rain*
21. *Firework*

ReSOURCES

Helpful websites

Unicode Consortium

The Unicode Consortium is the organisation that helps maintain, develop and promote software internationalisation standards and data.
» unicode.org

Unicode Emoji

As mentioned above, the Unicode Consortium is devoted to software internationalisation standards and data. The emoji section of the website gives information about Unicode emoji and its development. It also provides a handy list of all the latest emojis and external resources related to all things emoji.
» unicode.org/emoji/

Emojipedia

Emojipedia gives definitions of all current emojis. It also has a news blog so that you can keep up to date with all the latest emoji developments.
» emojipedia.org

Emoji Academy

Emoji Academy is a website with lots of fun features dedicated to the world of emojis—who doesn't want to make their own emoji print story?! The site is also jam-packed full of emoji information so you can keep learning about the latest emoji trends.
» emoji.academy

Online safety from NSPCC

It's very important to know how to stay safe online. There's a section of the NSPCC website that suggests lots of ways to browse the internet safely. You can also turn back to page 7 for some of our tips for staying safe online.
» nspcc.org.uk/preventing-abuse/keeping-children-safe/online-safety

INDeX

ILLUSTRATION CREDITS

Published by Collins
An imprint of HarperCollinsPublishers
Westerhill Road
Bishopbriggs
Glasgow G64 2QT
www.harpercollins.co.uk

In association with National Geographic
Partners, LLC

NATIONAL GEOGRAPHIC and the Yellow Border
Design are trademarks of the National
Geographic Society, used under license.

First published 2018

ISBN: 978-0-00-796501-4

10 9 8 7 6 5 4 3 2 1

A catalogue record for this book is available
from the British Library.

Printed in China by RR Donnelley APS Co Ltd.

If you would like to comment on any aspect
of this book, please contact us at the above
address or online.

natgeokidsbooks.co.uk
collins.reference@harpercollins.co.uk

Paper from responsible sources.